QUALITY AUDITS FOR IMPROVED PERFORMANCE

DENNIS R. ARTER, P.E.

QUALITY AUDITS FOR IMPROVED PERFORMANCE

DENNIS R. ARTER, P.E.

Library of Congress Cataloging-in-Publication Data

Arter, Dennis R.,
    Quality audits for improved performance.

    Bibliography: p.
    Includes index.
    1. Quality control—Auditing.   I.   Title
TS156.A76 1989   658.5'62   88-36256
ISBN 0-87389-057-4

Acquisitions Editor: Jeanine L. Lau
Production Editor: Tammy Griffin
Cover design by Artistic License. Set in Optima by
Carlisle Communications, Ltd. Printed and bound by Edwards Brothers.

ISBN 0-87389-057-4

ASQC Quality Press
611 East Wisconsin Avenue
Milwaukee, Wisconsin 53202

Printed in the United States of America

TABLE OF CONTENTS

FOREWORD

You are about to be introduced to some new and exciting approaches to the process of management audits. Historically, auditing has been the domain of accountants and IRS examiners. By examining past records in minute detail, their perceived goal has been to find errors. In today's environment of intense global competition, the old adversarial methods will no longer work. Using some of the basic accounting principles (thus the term *audit*), we can examine the usefulness and implementation of management control programs being practiced by business and government, but in a more positive manner. Management audits, along with financial audits, are now being used by most successful organizations as a means of determining whether control programs work effectively. Likewise, auditors are being drawn from all disciplines, including secretaries, social workers, and scientists.

ACKNOWLEDGMENTS

This text is based on nearly 20 years of experience in the quality sciences, most of which has involved auditing. Many of the management principles learned in the U.S. Navy nuclear submarine force are included in these pages. Basic auditing skills were developed, with some help from the existing consensus standards but mainly through trial and error, in the early days of Virginia Power's nuclear power station operations. Training of others in audit methods was originally accomplished by the author through means of a package course developed in 1978 by Mr. Frank X. Brown for the U.S. Department of Energy. Seeing a need for auditing in a nonregulated environment, a revision of Mr. Brown's course was made in the fall of 1984 in order to remove reference to nuclear activities and methods.

Membership in the Quality Auditing Technical Committee of the American Society for Quality Control has had a great deal of influence on the author's perception of many of the concepts presented herein. The area of auditing, in its many forms, is just beginning to be acknowledged by American business and government as a cost-effective means of improving quality. For this reason, several of the concepts discussed herein are new and controversial.

This text is a translation of actual practice and training course ideas into a nonclassroom environment. It is designed to be a basic resource to those contemplating a new quality audit program and those just beginning to practice the art of quality auditing.

CHAPTER 1

INTRODUCTION

What Is an Audit?

Although many people use the term *audit,* it seldom means the same thing in actual practice. This is because people use words based on their previous experiences or what they have read. Here are some definitions currently in use:

1. *Webster's New World Dictionary* defines audit as "A regular examination and checking of accounts or financial records; a settlement or adjustment of accounts; or a final statement of account." These definitions are principally structured around financial matters, and have limited application for the management examination process.

2. *Roget's Thesaurus* gives several synonyms for audit, among them being a check, inspection, and examination. Other terms sometimes used by quality assurance practitioners include review, appraisal, surveillance, and assessment.

3. The American Society for Quality Control (ASQC) defines a *quality audit* as "A systematic examination of the acts and decisions by people with respect to quality, in order to independently verify or evaluate and report compliance to the operational requirements of the quality program or the specification or contract requirements of the product or service." It is further stated that the intent of a quality audit is to conduct an independent review and evaluation so that needed corrective action can be obtained. A *quality system audit* is further defined as an independent assessment of the effectiveness of an organization's quality system.[1]

In general, there are four forms of audits, and each has its own applications and requirements. These are often referred to as financial audit, product audit, process audit, and systems audit. To understand and apply the principles of auditing, one must understand how each of these audits is used.

1

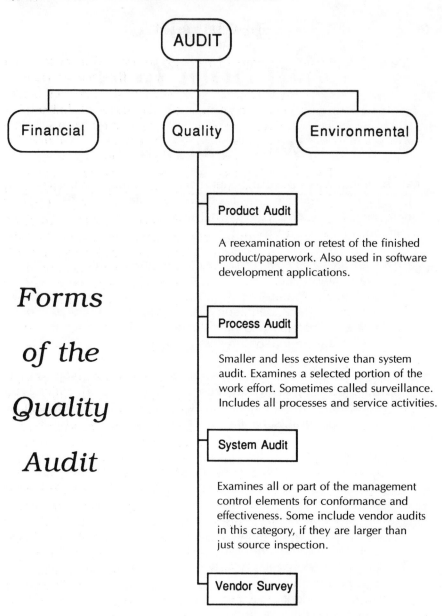

Forms

of the

Quality

Audit

AUDIT

Financial   **Quality**   **Environmental**

Product Audit

A reexamination or retest of the finished product/paperwork. Also used in software development applications.

Process Audit

Smaller and less extensive than system audit. Examines a selected portion of the work effort. Sometimes called surveillance. Includes all processes and service activities.

System Audit

Examines all or part of the management control elements for conformance and effectiveness. Some include vendor audits in this category, if they are larger than just source inspection.

Vendor Survey

Examination of a vendor's management of their quality effort to your existing or expected contractual requirements. Often included in the system audit category.

Financial Audits

Financial audits are performed by personnel trained in accounting processes. Their primary purpose is to verify that the accounting methods within an organization are giving the directors and stockholders a true representation of the financial status of that organization. This is not a trivial matter, in that large sums of money are dependent on the truthfulness of the financial statement. Additionally, firms must always be looking for waste, fraud, and abuse. The financial audit helps to satisfy these two needs. Financial auditors are normally certified public accountants (CPAs). They either belong to the internal audit group and report to the chief financial officer of the firm or agency, or they work for an accounting firm contracted to perform independent outside audits. Although quality auditing methods have their roots in financial auditing, they cover a much broader spectrum than just the financial records and accounts. This text will not cover financial auditing. Those interested in the area of financial audits may wish to contact the Institute of Internal Auditors or read one of the many texts on this subject.[2,3]

Product Audits

A product audit is a detailed examination of some finished product prior to acceptance by the purchaser. In such an inspection, actual physical attributes (dimensions, paint coverage, electrical resistance, etc.) may be measured and verified for conformance with fabrication documents. For a computer software job, sections of a module might be checked against programming standards. The various papers and certifications are gathered and examined to see if they agree with procurement specifications. The entire package is then assembled and accepted so that the product may be shipped. Another form of product audit might be to choose a finished item from the end of the process line and verify that it is in total agreement with all the affected specifications. A product audit does not examine the total management picture. It may be performed by a skilled technician with little or no supervision, as the requirements are relatively clear-cut. Product auditors are usually senior QC technicians. Because of its limited scope, the product audit will not be discussed further.

Process Audits

The process audit examines an activity to verify that the inputs, processing, and outputs are being performed in accordance with defined requirements. It usually covers only a portion of the total process and should take a relatively short period of time. Otherwise, it would be called 100 percent inline inspection, something industry stopped doing with the advent of World War II. This type of audit is a check of conformance of the process, operators, and equipment to defined requirements. It examines the adequacy and effectiveness of the process controls over the equipment and operators as established by procedures, work instructions, and process sheets. Many organizations refer to a process audit as a *surveillance,* to distinguish it from the much larger management audit. This text will follow that convention. A surveillance may be performed by an experienced inspector, technician, or engineer and is usually completed in less than two hours. The results of this short process examination are reported in something less than one page. As more firms move away from inspection and toward audit, the process audit (surveillance) becomes an important tool in the achievement of quality.

Systems Audits

A systems audit is known by several other names. Among these are management audit, systems and procedures audit, operational audit, and various substitutions of the terms *review* and *survey* for the word *audit.* It is characterized by its objective of examining the bigger picture of the organization. The two basic forms of this type of audit are internal and external. The former examines the management methods within a company or agency, while the latter looks at the contractors, vendors, and suppliers. Some also choose to further divide the external audit into *vendor survey* and *vendor audit,* where the survey is performed before the contract is let and is a best-guess of contractor performance based upon work in progress for other customers.

Common Traits

Despite the differences in application for these four forms of an *audit,* they all have several things in common. First, they are performed on a selected portion of something. One does not audit every financial transaction, every valve shipped, every mustard jar filled, or every management action. An audit selects a portion of the available universe to examine and then draws certain conclusions on the whole. Second, all audits require some sort of requirement, specification, or other such measuring criteria. They need some standard of performance. An efficiency review may be beneficial, but it cannot be termed an audit. Finally, all audits are performed by someone other than the performer of the activity under examination. This gives an audit a certain degree of independence and thus respect in the eyes of the user of the audit report.

Promises

As used in this text, an *audit* is a formal evaluation of performance to predetermined standards and the presentation of that evaluation in such a manner that change is induced toward *IMPROVED PERFORMANCE*. It's a structured means of measuring the conformance of actions to promises. As many in the quality and management fields have shown, unless one can measure a process, it becomes difficult to change that process for the better. It should be noted that the term *process* here is not limited to the traditional manufacturing definition. It means any structured means of accomplishing an objective.

An important difference in this definition for audit lies in the term *promises*. Organizations make such promises everyday. Examples include:

- Promises to employees in the form of company policies

- Promises to department heads and fellow workers in the form of company procedures

- Promises to the regulators in the form of licenses

- Promises to customers in the form of contracts and purchase orders

- Promises to consumers in the form of advertising

- Promises to the public in the form of Impact Statements and community commitments

If any of these promises are not kept, the group has lost credibility and the success of the company or mission may be in jeopardy.

Management Principles

Regardless of the goods or services produced, all management systems include these four fundamental activities:

Planning

The activities to be performed should be planned before they happen. Responsibilities must be set so that accountability and ownership of resulting performance is established. The identity and needs of the customer should be defined. Requirements should be specified in written documents which are used to describe the work activity or products ordered. All this becomes the requirements base against which quality is measured.

Performance

The action should proceed as planned. Records should be kept so that measurement can take place. Those performing the tasks should be given the proper tools and training to accomplish the job as specified.

The Quality Cycle

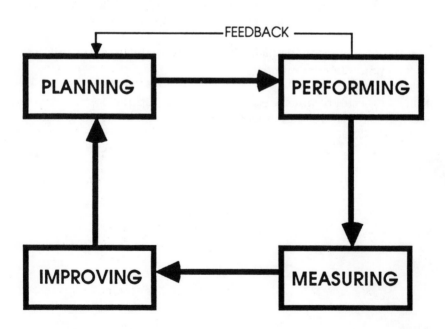

Measurement

The success (or failure) of an activity needs to be measured against some accepted standard. Tools used include inspection, surveillance, audit, appraisal, and review. All involved in the activity should be aware of the quality as measured. Feedback from the customer is vital to success.

Improvement

Problems must be corrected and the process improved. Managers and workers can share concepts for improvement, but the ultimate responsibility for such improvement rests with management. Changes should be communicated to the customer.

Because good quality is produced by good management, these are the fundamental building blocks for a quality assurance (QA) program. Historically, the term *quality assurance* has been associated with things like checks, audits, inspections, and other forms of verification. It is now recognized that quality and productivity cannot be inspected in; they must be managed in. Managers select people capable of creating a good product or service. They then ensure that the employees are properly trained, equipped, motivated, and supervised to achieve the desired product quality. Using the framework of a quality assurance system, managers can perform their traditional duties of planning, organizing, directing, and controlling.

The Role of the Audit Function

The fundamental role of the QA organization is to act as an extension of management by:

- Monitoring the overall performance of the company, plant, or agency

- Identifying substandard or anomalous performance, or precursors of potential problems

- Reporting their findings in an understandable form in a timely fashion to a level of management having authority to effect corrective action

- Promptly verifying the effectiveness of the corrective action and reporting those results back to management.

7

These are also traits found in any good auditing system, whether it be for financial accountability, productivity, or quality.

Why Audit?

One reason for auditing is for survival. In any competitive situation, business will go to the more efficient provider. If you do not know how well (or poorly) your organization is performing, someone will take your business away. Federal, state, and city government agencies are also affected, in that programs funded can be dropped when objectives are not achieved. Quality has become the key to survival in our competitive world-class marketplace. To have only half of a program to enhance that quality is shortchanging both providers and receivers of a product or service.

Another reason for conducting audits lies in many of the regulations imposed on your operations. In today's environment, there is no such thing as a nonregulated concern. For example, in order to get and keep a license to operate and maintain a nuclear power plant, the parties involved must develop and implement a rigorous program of external and internal audits. Likewise, the Federal Aviation Administration requires audits by airplane manufacturers and users to provide assurance that safety is not being compromised. The Food and Drug Administration requires a program of audits and other forms of monitoring for those firms licensed to produce and sell drugs and medical devices. Most of the contracts written by the U.S. Defense Department require the contractor to implement an approved program of internal and external auditing.

A third reason to conduct quality management audits is to counter the actions of outsiders opposed to what you may be doing. For one reason or another, powerful organizations that you have no control over are continually looking for the errors and mistakes you will make. Everyone will make these errors; the smart ones will discover such mistakes when they are small and relatively easy to correct. If you do not care enough to monitor your controls, outsiders may assume that obligation for you. Often, their reports may use tactics that could be damaging to your mission. If you can show the outsiders that you have an effective program, they will be more inclined to leave you alone.

A Different Philosophy

When you perform audits, you must reflect on the needs of your customers—those managers desiring the audit in the first place. Like many other service groups, you have a variety of users of your product. The ASQC consensus standard on auditing, ANSI/ASQC Q1–1986, refers to the formal customer of the audit as the *client*.[1] This is typically the QA manager, acting as a resource for the line managers who direct the production of marketable goods or services or are directly accountable for the mission of a government agency. In a way, the people being audited are also your customers, in that they will benefit from an unbiased and thorough review and analysis of their operations. For supplier audits, the end users of the purchased goods and services are your customers.

To be useful to your customers, audits must be performed and presented in a meaningful fashion. Peter Drucker, the well-known management expert and author of several books on management principles, has said that workers work in the system, while managers work on the system. In order for the affected managers to work on the process being audited, the bottom line must be in management's terms and appeal to their interests. Do they really care if six drawings are missing review signatures? So what? If, however, your audit is performed such that a projection of the continued practice of not documenting drawing reviews shows that the quality of the product is or could be adversely affected, then the responsible managers can take steps to correct the situation. Or perhaps this was just a bad day for an otherwise excellent employee, and represents no real threat. Management can turn its attention to more important matters.

A different perspective for management-type audits is needed. Instead of examining past conformance to requirements and regulations in minute detail, you can use current performance to project future actions. It is better to avoid dwelling on mistakes of the past. They can never be changed. A backward looking view cannot achieve the goal of improved performance within the organization being examined. It will only lead to antagonism and backstabbing. This is because people are powerless to change the past. They become frustrated and strike back, usually at you. Instead, use past practices to predict future performance, which can be changed.

Modern management audits should be a combination of compliance and effectiveness evaluations. Using defined and agreed-to measurement criteria, the audit report will tell managers:

- Whether control programs are being implemented

- Whether control programs really work

The only way to successfully meet these two needs is to thoroughly prepare for the audit, conduct the review with a high degree of professionalism, and present the report in terms meaningful to management. Then affected managers using the information presented by your audit will be able to make changes to improve future performance.

Footnotes

[1]ANSI/ASQC Standard Q1–1986 *Generic Guidelines for Auditing of Quality Systems*.

[2]Institute of Internal Auditors, 249 Maitland Avenue, P.O. Box 1119, Altamonte Springs, FL 32715, 407/830–7600.

[3]Sawyer, L. B. *The Practice of Modern Internal Auditing, ed 2*. Altamonte Springs, FL, Institute of Internal Auditors, 1981.

CHAPTER 2

ADMINISTRATION

The Overall Plan

Appropriate management, both quality and line, must do some basic planning to determine what activities should be audited regardless of the actual schedule. These activities include internal functions performed by various groups within an organization, and external functions performed by contractors, suppliers, or other outside groups.

One way some companies do this is to set up a matrix that shows all groups, such as projects, product lines, and/or processes, along one axis and the commitments made along the other axis. This provides a start for planning audits, whether by commitments across organizational groups or by the groups themselves. A similar list may be prepared for external audits. List critical vendors along one axis and the groups or product lines served by those vendors along the other axis. Remember though, not all suppliers need the attention that an audit demands. Sometimes an occasional inspection at the plant or warehouse is sufficient. Often, a simple receiving inspection of incoming items will suffice.

Scheduling Audits

Management, usually the audit boss or QA manager, should develop an annual audit schedule based on the overall wish list just described. Because we can never perform all of the audits we would like, the schedule must consider resources available and product or project schedules. That is, audits should be scheduled at times when activities can be observed, rather than be limited to auditing just records. Another factor to be considered is the "health" of the control programs being considered, meaning that audits should be scheduled, or added to the preplanned schedule, more frequently for areas with known problems. An objective should be to audit all activities, within some time frame, in sufficient depth to make certain that the entire management control program is being implemented effectively. This means that those activities that are critical to safety, reliability, or profitability, should be audited more often than those that are relatively less important.

Once the annual schedule is developed, it should receive wide distribution among senior management, so that all know when their audits are coming. Of course, the schedule will require modification occasionally to include new information, changes in project or vendor status, and special management requests. Care should be taken to keep all managers apprised of these changes.

A detailed audit planning schedule should then be developed, probably on a quarterly cycle. Typically found within the detailed audit schedule is information such as:

- Audited activity

- Start date

- Audit team leader

It is most important that all affected managers of the audited groups receive a copy of this schedule. The contracts people should also alert affected vendors. Remember, there is still a great deal of fear attached to the concept of auditing because of unpleasant experiences. If an external or internal group is going to oppose the performance of an audit on them, it is best to define that opposition early and allow the parties to negotiate.

Auditor Qualification

Auditors must be trained and qualified to perform their examinations and analyses. There are two levels of qualification, auditor and lead auditor. Both levels should be supported by written qualification records. Lead auditors organize and direct the audit, report audit results, and evaluate the resulting corrective action. On the other hand, auditors participate in the audit process. They are typically technical specialists, management representatives, new auditors-in-training, and, of course, other auditors and lead auditors assigned to the team.

Auditors perform their assigned portion of the audit only under the supervision of a lead auditor. In Chapter 3 the reasons why are discussed. Because of this closeness to the leader, it is relatively easy to qualify a prospective auditor. Typically this is accomplished by one or more of the following methods:

- Orientation to provide an understanding of the products, goods, or services being provided by the organization to be audited, along with an understanding of the expected methods to be evaluated.

- Participation in training programs designed to provide knowledge of the audit process. Such training might include audit objectives, team assignments, conduct of audits, how to report results, and expectations for documenting the process.

- On-the-job training, guidance, and counseling by a qualified lead auditor. Of course, all expected tasks should be included in such training.

Lead Auditors

Lead auditors are significantly harder to qualify. The lead auditor must have the demonstrated ability to extract information, analyze that information, and report the results in a meaningful fashion. This requires the possession of communication skills, formal training, audit participation, and an examination for competency.

Communication Skills

To perform the task of auditing, the lead auditor must be able to extract and provide information. Each requires the ability to communicate effectively both orally and in writing. Clear and simple reports are the mark of a good lead auditor.[1,2] The ability to present complex issues to an often hostile audience is another mark of a good lead auditor. Finally, the lead auditor must be able to receive information from others. This requires the ability to read and listen effectively.

Formal Training

The prospective lead auditor should receive formal training to provide a base on which to perform audits. Such training should include topics on the control methods (codes, standards, commitments) being examined, the goods and/or services being provided, the general principles of quality assurance, and the specific techniques of audit planning, performance, reporting, and followup. Several commercial courses are presented around the nation to fulfill this training for various interest groups. Additionally, many firms develop their own in-house training program and include auditor training as one of the offerings.

Experience

The prospective lead auditor needs to be able to try out various classroom theories in the real world in order to adapt them to his or her own approaches. This should be done under the direction of a qualified lead auditor, or at least a member of the management team if no lead auditors exist. Companies typically require that at least five audits be performed under instruction within the past three years, in order to meet their audit participation requirement.

Examination

An objective and documented examination of the prospective lead auditor's capabilities is the final step in qualification. Of course, a written examination is preferred, but an oral examination will do. Many organizations find a qualification board to be a useful approach. Two to four experienced auditors, managers, quality engineers, etc. sit around a table and quiz the potential lead auditor on various aspects of auditing and reactions to potential situations.

Certification

Upon completion of the final examination, the individual may be certified as a lead auditor by his or her management. It is important that such certification come from the employer. If third-party certifications are used, they should supplement, not take the place of, examination and analysis by the employer. The lead auditor certification record should include:

- Identification of the employer

- The lead auditor's name

- The date of certification/recertification

- The basis of the qualification, such as communication skills, formal training, experience, and examination

- The signature of the person doing the certifying

Lead auditors need to maintain their qualification through regular and active participation in the audit process. If a person has not performed an audit within the past year, it would be appropriate to require some sort of refresher training before he or she was assigned to lead another audit. Note that participation does not necessarily mean that the person must have performed as a lead auditor within the past year. The important issue is to not allow auditing skills to become rusty.

Formal Audit Procedures

Formal plans and procedures for the audit program are needed in order to provide structure and quality to the audit product. In addition, fear of the audit process by potential auditees will be reduced if the rules are known. Procedures should be developed in a spirit of co-operation between all departments and should not be commandments from the auditing group. Areas to consider when developing audit procedures include:

- Methods for determining areas to be audited and proposed schedules, including the means of revising these plans.

- Methods for preparing for audits, including team composition and training, notification of affected parties, and checklist development.

- Methods for performing audits and how data will be recorded and communicated during the audit process.

- Methods for reporting audit results, including measures to take when serious deficiencies are discovered.

- Methods to be used for tracking and closing resulting corrective action measures.

These procedures (or procedure) should cover external audits of suppliers or vendors as well as internal audits of your own operations. An approach for the latter is presented in Appendix 1.

Summary

An effective audit program needs a firm basis which should include good scheduling, qualification of auditors, and sound procedures. Chapter 3 presents some detail on how to initiate the audit and perform the necessary up-front planning.

Footnotes

[1]An excellent source of information on clear and effective writing is the Document Design Center, American Institutes for Research, 3333 K Street, NW, Washington, DC 20007. They also publish a newsletter called *Simply Stated.*

[2]The U.S. Air Force has also published a book called *Tongue and Quill* which is available from the Superintendent of Documents, U.S. Government Printing Office, Washington, DC 20402. Ask for Air Force Pamphlet 13–2 of January 1985.

CHAPTER 3
PREPARATION

Phases of the Audit Process

Quality auditing may be divided into four phases, progressing sequentially through the process:

- The *preparation phase* of an audit starts from the assignment of a particular audit to a lead auditor and includes all activities from the time that a team is selected up to the on-site gathering of information.

- The *performance phase* begins with the opening meeting with the auditee and includes the gathering of information and analysis of that information. Normally this is accomplished by conducting interviews and examining records.

- The *reporting phase* covers the translation of the audit team conclusions into a tangible product. It includes the exit meeting with the auditee and publication of the formal audit report.

- The *closure phase* of the audit deals with the actions resulting from the report and the documentation of the entire audit effort. For audits resulting in the identification of some weakness, the closure phase includes tracking and evaluating the followup action taken by others to fix the problem and keep it from repeating. Typically this is referred to as "corrective action."

Steps in the Preparation Phase

Between the time you receive an assignment and the time the audit starts, there are many things to be done to lay the foundation and properly organize the work. The experienced auditor probably does it routinely from habit. The novice tends to do a great deal of fumbling in an audit before getting down to the actual surveys and examinations. To minimize such fumbling, you should use the nine steps for audit preparation: (1) define the purpose of the audit, (2) define the scope of the audit, (3) determine the resources to be applied, (4) identify the authority for the audit, (5) identify the performance standards to be used, (6) contact the auditee, (7) develop written checklists, (8) review performance history of the auditee, and (9) develop an initial understanding of the control systems.

While each audit is likely to be different from the others, these steps are common to all, regardless of whether you are performing product, process, systems, or supplier audits. Just as airline pilots use a preflight checklist to verify that all items have been accomplished prior to takeoff, you may need to list a check before your own "takeoff." Such a reminder list is not designed to inhibit your creativity; it will merely make the planning easier. Any format will do nicely, as long as it contains the items to be accomplished and some due dates. Once the list is prepared, you may proceed with an assurance that important items will not be forgotten.

Purpose

"What do your customers want to achieve with the audit?" The answer to this question is critically important to the success of an audit and, thus, improved performance. As mentioned earlier, the users of your audit are those managers producing the product or service which makes the venture profitable, or in the case of government, those managers charged with implementing the agency's mission to the public. Audits are not performed for the quality department.

Do these users of the audit wish to determine whether a vendor's quality assurance program complies with the requirements of some standard? Do they wish to evaluate the effectiveness of a process control sheet designed to eliminate scrap? Does your company (agency) wish to know whether established procedures are being carried out, to evaluate the effectiveness of those procedures, or both? The answers to these and similar questions are used to develop the purpose statement. Experience has shown that management audits are most beneficial when used to determine both the compliance with, and the effectiveness of, existing control methods. Your clients truly wish to know whether controls are being followed and whether those controls are working as planned. Once you have determined the purpose of the audit, write it down. Normally, the purpose statement is one sentence long.

Scope

Your next step in the preparation phase is to establish the scope of the audit. The scope establishes a perimeter around the area to be audited and identifies the items, groups, and activities to be examined. Defining the scope also helps to make the most efficient use of limited audit resources.

The scope of an audit will vary considerably. Examples for a typical internal audit by a manufacturing company might be:

- Broad Brush—all control methods for a product line

- Total System—procurement activities for all products

- Part of a System—receiving activities within procurement

For external audits of an existing supplier, the scope is usually easy to define—performance to your contract by the vendor. They may be doing work for others too, but your audit should examine performance for your firm. If you don't have a contract yet, then the audit (sometimes called a survey) can only examine the performance of similar work being done for others.

The scope of an audit has a great deal of effect on its length. If the scope is too large, the audit cannot possibly be completed in a reasonable time. Conversely, too narrow a scope will waste valuable resources. In addition, economics and personnel availability must be considered when developing the scope. Audits of greater than one week's duration for the performance (data gathering) phase are normally excessive. When planning audits, one should also consider the time resources of the people being audited. Remember, production and routine staff assignments are seriously affected by the disruptive environment of the typical audit.

Keeping track of the audit scope may be one of the more challenging tasks for the audit team and particularly the team leader. Often during the course of an audit, additional areas in need of examination appear which may be outside of the original scope of the audit. The team must ask itself whether the concern is important enough to pursue immediately (without the normal preparation), or whether it can wait for a separate examination at a later date. The responsibility for this decision lies with the team leader, after consulting headquarters.

Generally, it's best to stick to the original scope, regardless of what develops. The auditors are perceived as more credible when they stick to the rules.

Does this mean that the audit team should ignore a serious deficiency, uncovered during the course of their audit, just because it lies outside of the current scope? Of course not. You should proceed as you would under a nonaudit situation. Use the established methods already in place, like problem report, nonconformance report, or trouble desk, to report the condition to those managers that are affected. You have done your duty and can now proceed with the audit as planned.

The Audit Team

In theory, the next step is to select the audit team, based on the purpose and scope just developed. In practice, the resources of the audit group will often determine the purpose and scope. Only so many audits can be performed by a staff of two. Only so many vendors can be examined when travel funds are limited.

One-person audits are an invitation to trouble. To prevent the audit from becoming a narrow interpretation of existing standards or methods, the team should be composed of at least two individuals. No matter how well you plan or how clear the standards appear, auditing will always require some interpretation. A single auditor will eventually "steer" the entire company or agency down his or her path of goodness. While you may be blessed with a talented auditor, eventually this single perspective will cause pain. The team approach encourages balance and will be assumed for the duration of this text. Any team with more than six members, however, becomes a mob. It cannot be controlled effectively, even by the experienced team leader.

If possible, someone from outside of the QA organization should be on the audit team to further the concept of balance. Although it is common for the team leader to be a member of the quality group, audit team members are drawn from all departments within an organization. An engineer or technician from a related discipline makes an ideal team member, as they often see the controls being examined from a different perspective and become champions for the quality assurance program after the audit is finished. Senior secretaries make great auditors when properly directed. They know "bosses' language" and the real way things are run, not just the documented ways found in procedures. Many firms are going so far as to require a technical representative and management representative on each internal QA audit performed.

In order for the audit to be effective and successful (i.e., improve performance), the audit team members must be trained. A common mistake is for a new employee in the QA group to be designated as the "Company Cop," under the premise that one can learn the company culture by monitoring it. Wrong! Such an arrangement violates several sound management principles. It allows a neophyte to cause untold disruptions and errors throughout the audit process and it further antagonizes the line folks against the quality organization.

In addition to the rules and procedures, auditors must be knowledgeable of the process to be audited. They should know something about the product line and who the customers are. Every group has customers, either external or internal, and the audit team should explore these relationships. Auditors should be humanists as opposed to technologists; after all, it's the human element being examined, not a bunch of printed circuit boards.

Authority

The next step in the preparation phase is to determine the authority for the audit. In far too many cases, extensive preparation was wasted when the potential audit team discovered they were not welcome or even allowed into the plant. They had assumed that the necessary authority to conduct the audit existed. Another reason for identifying the authority to audit is to defuse that natural human reaction by the auditee to become defensive when informed of a forthcoming audit. Managers may develop the opinion that they are being harassed or "picked on." By specifying the authority for the audit to all involved parties (including your client and other users of the audit), you confer legitimacy to the audit and remove (or minimize) those adverse feelings.

For vendor, supplier, and contractor audits, this authority is usually found in the contract or specification clauses, oftentimes under the "rights of access" heading. Government agencies often include standard "boilerplate" in the agreements for receipt of grants and contracts.[1] For internal audits, the authority is normally found in your company/agency quality assurance manual or similar policy document.

Performance Standards

Standards are the norms or criteria against which the performance of an activity is measured. These come from a variety of sources, depending upon the product or service involved. Sometimes these standards may be developed by a voluntary group of individuals under the sponsorship of a professional society, like the American Society for Quality Control (ASQC), and imposed upon the work by contract, specification, or procedure reference. The standard may come from a government agency, like the Department of Defense and their "MIL" standards. An industry association may develop standards as "rules" for belonging, such as hospital accreditation. Of course the basic purchase order, contract, or specification becomes a performance standard when you have a specific customer. Standards may also come from within, like the company policy and procedures manual, the manufacturing instructions, or the process sheets. Regardless of the source, standards represent proven methods of accomplishing the task with the desired control. They represent agreement between the desires of your client and the promises of the auditee.

As an example, the military often uses the specification MIL-Q-9858A, *Quality Program Requirements* for goods and services bought for use by the various armed forces.[2] Contractor, subcontractor, and supplier quality-related activities are measured against this and other applicable standards. The contractor's, subcontractor's, and supplier's quality program plans or manuals are also considered performance standards. For this example, MIL Q 9858A is the performance standard against which the contractor's overall quality program might be measured. Their company quality program then becomes the performance standard against which departmental level procedures, instructions, and other documents are measured. These procedures, instructions, and other documents become the standard against which the actual performance of work (or product) is measured. The lowest level standard might be the welding process specification used to fabricate some pipe. Thus, performance standards have many levels, and all should be identified.

Performance standards need to be clear, concise, and unambiguous; and they should not be subject to wide variations in interpretation. The lower the level of performance standard (like the welding specification just mentioned), the more quantitative they tend to become. For most audits, regardless of the purpose and scope, you will need access to these lower level standards (manuals, procedures, instructions, product specifications, and sometimes even blueprints) prior to the actual audit. They should be identified and copies acquired early in the preparation phase. Ask for them!

It should be emphasized that, without performance standards, there can be no meaningful measurement. And without measurement, audits become conjecture and not fact.

Initial Contact

After you have established the purpose, scope, resources, authority, and performance standards for the audit, the next step in the preparation phase is to make initial contact with the auditee.[3] Custom, as well as common courtesy, requires the auditee to be notified prior to beginning the on-site data gathering portion of the audit. The purpose of this initial contact is to inform the auditee that an audit will be conducted and also to inform them as to the purpose and scope of that audit. Of course, verbal communication prior to the formal announcement is certainly appropriate. This informal action is normally accomplished in person or over the telephone by the team leader. In the case of a vendor audit, all communication may be required to go through the buyer or contracting officer. Check the contract.

It is during this informal contact that a copy of the auditee's formal control methods (like the quality assurance manual or the engineering department procedures) and an organization chart are requested. Process specifications and product descriptions may also be appropriate. From this material, you should be able to identify the auditee's internal performance standards and procedures that apply to the audit scope. Further communication with the auditee may be necessary to identify these pertinent internal documents. Once they are identified, copies should be obtained, through the team leader or other designated person, as appropriate, for use in preparing the audit checklist.

Administrative details should also be worked out with the auditee. These include schedules, arrangements, and assignments. Mutually acceptable dates for the audit should be established so that the right people will be available during the audit period. Little good would result from an audit of the research department which was scheduled when most of the scientists were attending an important topical conference in Miami. A good rule here is to be firm but flexible.

Formal Notification

After these initial, informal details have been agreed to, a formal notification must still be sent to the auditee. This applies to both internal as well as external audits. Standard practice within most companies or agencies requires this formal notice to be delivered at least 30 days before beginning the performance phase. This forces the auditors to become better prepared and it gives the auditee sufficient time to prepare. Common practice is for the formal notice to come from the manager requesting the audit (the client); although, in some cases, the notification must come from the contracting officer or other contracting representative. This is an effective way to give the client *ownership* of the audit and keeps them actively involved in the whole process. Since you want your audit to address management issues, the notification letter or memo should aim for the top. Keep this in mind when you are asked to draft one. It should go to the senior manager in actual charge of the area of interest. For internal audits, this might be a department head or project manager. For vendor audits, it would probably be the company president or division manager.

The following items should be contained in the notification letter or memorandum:

- Audited organization

- Purpose of the audit

- Scope of the audit

- Performance standards

- Activities to be audited

- Any interfacing organizations requiring notification

- Applicable background documents

- Identification of the audit team members

- Preliminary schedule for the audit

Whether these items are contained within the letter or memo, or listed on a separate audit plan attached to a cover letter or memo should be determined by the preference of your local management.

The important thing is that these items are formally addressed and communicated to all parties before the audit investigations start.

Surveillances

Because the surveillance (process audit) often consists of an examination of the same activities over a period of time, notification of the auditee to the extent just described is rarely appropriate for each surveillance conducted. It is, however, appropriate to notify the auditee before beginning a surveillance program. Items like purpose, scope, and standards should be initially identified, so that the people subject to surveillance will know what to expect. If this is done in the form of a detailed surveillance instruction or procedure for the individual affected process areas, then the 30-day criteria is easy to meet.

Audit Checklists

You will be expected to examine all of the selected control areas identified from the various performance standards chosen for your audit. Additionally, a method is needed for organizing all the documents and working papers which together will form the final records of the audit. An effective audit checklist will meet both of these needs. Not only is a checklist recommended, it is required by several audit program standards. A checklist is also one of the distinguishing differences between an audit and other, less formal, methods of performance monitoring. This checklist serves as a guide to each member of the audit team, in order to assure that the full scope of the audit is adequately covered. It also provides a place for the documentation of each auditor's examination of evidence.

Contents of the Checklist

There are certain criteria which any audit checklist should include, regardless of the audit subject or scope. Obviously, the checklist must first provide for clear identification of the specific audit topic or subject to which it applies, the activity or organization to be audited, and the audit dates. A unique reference number may be assigned to your audit and this, too, will be identified in the heading information of the checklist.

The main function of the checklist is to list the specific points to be examined. The format by which this is accomplished will vary from organization to organization. Some choose to list the questions in a column down the left side of the page. This is followed by a center column for checking "yes/no" or "sat/unsat," and another column on the right side for recording the objective evidence examined for that question. Others choose to simply list the questions on the page with an inch or two of white space between questions for recording notes and reference to objective evidence. Either format is acceptable.

The checklist should have a cross-reference to the specific section of the standard which established that requirement. These cross-references not only provide you with a handy reply to the question, "Where did that requirement come from?" but they also force precision in the development of the checklist in the first place.

It is also necessary to include a plan for collection of specific evidence needed to answer certain checklist questions. What do you wish to look at? How many items do you want to sample? These are the types of questions that should be addressed in the checklist. Naturally, you won't know all of the places to look prior to the audit, but you should be aware of some.

An audit checklist should provide you with space for recording the results of your examinations, including an identification of those people you talked with. As mentioned previously, some people prefer columns for entering data and interview results, while others prefer white space between individual questions. You should use the format that works best for you, as these become your notes and the success of the audit may depend upon how well you can reconstruct an interview or document check.

Standardized Checklists

Some organizations like to use "canned" checklists, which are available from various sources. These standard checklists are of the "one size fits all" variety. By themselves, they are not useful for performance improvement audits because they do not reflect how any particular organization assigns responsibilities and authority, they fail to identify some special features of a particular control system that may be crucial to success, and, they may address only a few of the performance criteria. Additionally, they allow the audit to proceed without really adequate preparation and thought. The use of standard checklists by themselves is not recommended. However, they can provide the auditors with a bank of potential questions upon which to draw. This approach is encouraged. Likewise, you should save questions used on previous audits for potential application to the current audit. With the advent of microcomputers, along with word processing software, use of these banks of questions can significantly reduce checklist preparation time.[4]

Preparation of the Checklists

It is normally the responsibility of each audit team member to prepare specific checklist questions appropriate to their assigned portion of the audit. For example, one individual might be assigned to examine "document control," another to "control of the computer source code library," and a third to "configuration control of drill bits." Each individual would identify specific requirements applicable to the assigned area, and enter them onto a checklist.

One approach often used for the development of checklist questions is to separate each requirement paragraph of the standard into smaller, manageable "bits," then rephrase those requirements in the form of questions needing a "yes" or "no" answer. These are intended as questions for you to answer after review of the procedures, completion of interviews, and examination of evidence. In other words, you must determine whether the auditee does or does not meet requirements. When preparing your checklist questions, you must be careful not to change the essential requirements of the standard by careless use of similar words, as you have no authority for rewording a requirement to reflect your own bias or preferred way of accomplishing a task. A simple technique for preventing such error is the cut-and-paste method; simply cut words or phrases from a copy of the requirement document, and paste them onto the checklist.

When finished with the checklist development, each auditor should submit his or her portion to peer review. This serves as a check of thoroughness, proper logic construction, and absence of bias. Any qualified reviewer will do. This may be the lead auditor, another team member, or the manager of the auditing section. The purpose of this review should not be to approve your checklist, but rather, subject it to a critical examination of content. Better checklists and thus better audits will result from this practice. Once done, the review should be recorded somewhere so that you may take credit for it. Usually, a signature and date at the bottom of the first page of the checklist is satisfactory.

History

In developing the checklists and preparing for the audit, it helps to know the history of past performance by the auditee. Your organization may have performed a previous audit in this or a similar area.

In such a case, you should review records of prior audits and identify from these records any specific area likely to have continuing or repeat problems. Add this information to the audit checklist. If the prior audit revealed any noncompliance to requirements, you should determine the current status of actions that were taken to resolve the noncompliance. The previous audit team leader may have closed out these items based on information that specific corrective actions were implemented. The new audit team should verify that these actions have remained in effect, and that they have been effective in preventing recurrence of the problem or noncompliance.

For supplier audits, your procurement files may be a good source of information. Look for an excessive number of change orders or contract modifications. These could indicate some areas to investigate. This is a good time to discuss the supplier's performance with the users of their goods and services. These users may have particular areas of interest that merit examination by the audit team. Also, they are the ones that stand to gain the most by improved performance.

Evaluate

As discussed earlier, copies of the auditee's plans, procedures, and process descriptions should be requested during the initial contact discussions. Once obtained, each audit team member should examine these documents for two purposes: (1) to determine whether these documented instructions adequately respond to identified requirements of any higher-level performance standards; and (2) to obtain a better understanding of the auditee's activity so that the performance phase of the audit can be completed in an efficient and effective manner.

Entries should be made at this time in the appropriate sections of the audit checklist to indicate adequacy of the procedures under examination. If the written plan or procedure seems vague in its application of the control requirement, then mark your checklist accordingly; you will need to examine these areas in greater detail later on. Also, your study of the procedures will identify specific records, forms, or reports which are used to implement the required action. These should also be noted in the audit checklist, along with identification of the person or place where copies should be available. All of this effort will lead to a much greater understanding of the way the various control systems are designed to work. Your job in the performance part of the audit will become easier and considerably more enjoyable.

Information Sources

As you review the formal and documented control methods to be examined, you should be aware of the various types of evidence which might be used to verify implementation of the various promises. Evidence can be defined as facts used by the auditor to define and understand actual practices in use. Evidence takes many different forms, including oral statements of the auditee, written communications, and observations by the auditor. Six types commonly used in audits include: (1) physical examination, (2) confirmation, (3) documentation, (4) observation, (5) questions to the auditee, and (6) comparisons and relationships.

Physical Examination

Physical examination is the inspection or count by the auditor of tangible assets against established criteria. This type of evidence would most often be associated with products rather than services. Examples of physical examinations are:

1. Reinspection or retest of material accepted in the receiving department to verify that it meets acceptance criteria.

2. Rechecking measuring instruments after they have been calibrated to verify that the accuracy is within acceptable limits.

3. Reinspection or retest of a product after it has passed an inspection or test to verify that the item is acceptable.

Physical examination is regarded as one of the most reliable types of audit evidence. The auditee will have little difficulty relating to these tangible items when they are presented in the final report. However, this form of evidence should not be overused, as it tends to impart an aura of distrust.

Confirmation

Confirmation involves the receipt of a written response from an independent third party verifying the accuracy of some information. Analytical laboratories often use this method to verify that a particular testing process is still functioning properly. A sample is drawn and analyzed by both the laboratory and an outside agency. Then the two results are compared. Because confirmations come from sources independent of the auditee, they are highly regarded and believable.

However, confirmations are relatively costly to obtain and may cause some inconvenience to those asked to supply them. Therefore, they are not used in every instance in which they might be used. Whether confirmations are used depends on the reliability needs of the situation as well as the alternate evidence available.

Documentation

Documentation is the examination of recorded information (plans, procedures, instructions, specifications, reports, forms, drawings, records, etc.) to substantiate that something was performed and that it met requirements. Since many transactions and processes are often supported by at least one document, there is a large volume of this type of evidence available to you. Documentation is the most frequently used source of information, but it is also the most frequently abused. You must remember that all actions and activities are not, and should not be, recorded on a piece of paper.

Observation

Observation is the use of the senses to assess certain activities. Throughout an audit, there are many opportunities to use your sight, hearing, touch, and smell to evaluate a wide range of situations. For example, you may tour a vendor's plant to obtain a general impression of their facilities. You may observe that inventory parts are rusty or that noncomforming material is mixed in with conforming material. In-house, you may watch individuals performing certain tasks and notice a great deal of confusion in the data processing area. Observation is rarely sufficient by itself—it is necessary to follow up initial impressions with other kinds of corroborative evidence. Nevertheless, observation is useful in most parts of an audit.

Questions

This is the process of obtaining written or oral information from the auditee in response to your questions. Although considerable evidence is obtained from the auditee through inquiry, it cannot usually be regarded as conclusive because is it not from an independent source and may be biased in the auditee's favor. Therefore, when you gather facts this way, it is normally necessary to obtain further corroborating evidence by other means. As an example, if you wanted to obtain information about the data entry system, you would begin by asking someone how the system operates. Later, you perform or observe some data entry tests to determine if it indeed works in the way stated and is in accordance with the written procedures.

Comparisons

Comparisons and relationships are used primarily as a means of isolating activities that should be intensively investigated—those things that appear to be out of control. An example of this type of evidence would be to conduct a trend analysis on such things as the number of field support calls per month over the past year, to determine whether the rate for a certain model number is increasing or decreasing. Your own calculations, not those of the auditee, are generally used for comparisons and relationships. The tests should be performed early in the audit to aid in determining which areas should be more thoroughly investigated, and reviewed again at the end of the audit to corroborate the tentative conclusions reached on the basis of the other evidence.

Summary

These are the products of the preparation phase:

- An audit plan

- An audit checklist

- Arrangements made with the auditee

- An initial evaluation of the control methods

- A plan for the collecting of evidence

The audit plan will identify the organization to be audited, the subject or purpose of the audit and its scope, the activities to be audited, members of the audit team, and the documents (performance standards) applicable to the audit.

The audit checklist will identify the various items intended to be examined and the reference location for each requirement. It will show the kinds of evidence you plan to obtain during the audit. The checklist will contain space for recording your determination of compliance or noncompliance regarding each requirement bit checked, along with space to record comments and notes regarding certain conclusions. The checklist also identifies the activity to be audited, the auditor, audit date, personnel contacted during the audit, and the audit-identifying number.

The auditee has been informed of the audit, its purpose, scope, and authority. Mutually agreeable dates have been established for the audit and a rough audit schedule provided to the auditee. Copies of the various control documents and organization charts have been obtained, along with additional procedures and instructions applicable to this audit. Travel arrangements, including motel reservations, have been made if the audit is of another division or vendor outside of your immediate location.

From the review of the auditee's control methods and discussions with their customers, you have identified areas of probable strengths and weaknesses in the activity to be evaluated. You have also prepared a plan for collecting evidence. With the audit plan, audit schedule and partially completed checklist in hand, and with the necessary arrangements made, you are well on your way.

Footnotes

[1]From the Federal Acquisition Regulations, 48 CFR 52.246: "The Government has the right to inspect and test all supplies/services called for by the contract, to the extent practicable at all places and times during the term of the contract. The Government shall perform inspections and tests in a manner that will not unduly delay the work."

[2]Available free from the Naval Publications and Forms Center, 5801 Tabor Avenue, Philadelphia, PA 19120.

[3]On some occasions, "surprise" audits are appropriate and no specific notification would be given to the auditee. Situations where this might be appropriate include regulatory inspections and certain in-process inspections, where the primary purpose is to observe operations as they usually exist, rather than the "cleaned-up" state. In any case, the auditee should be aware of the possibility of a surprise or unannounced audit and what areas are to be examined.

[4]It should be recognized that standard checklists are appropriate for the surveillance program, where the same process is examined over time. Sometimes this is the only way trend data may be obtained. Likewise, certain product audits would benefit from the use of standard checklists, where several of the same type of item are to be examined. In either case, the checklists should be examined for potential changes after a period of use, such as once a quarter.

CHAPTER 4
PERFORMANCE

Performance Phase

The performance phase of an audit is known by many names such as fieldwork, examination, interviews, testing, and evaluation. It is the data-gathering portion of the audit and covers the time period from arrival at the audit location up to, but not including, the exit meeting. The performance phase consists of the following:

- An opening meeting

- Understanding the control system

- Verification of the control system

- Team and auditee meetings

Each of these activities will be explored in greater detail so that you gain a better understanding of the skills and mechanics of successful auditing.

Opening Meeting

All audits must have some sort of opening meeting in order to establish the face-to-face bond that will develop between the audit team members and the audited group.[1] The opening meeting, sometimes called an *entrance meeting,* is held soon after your arrival at the audit site, which may be a vendor plant or it may be with the folks down the hall. You should have the entire audit team at the meeting, so that they may each see and be seen. The team leader normally chairs the meeting, which should be brief. Elaborate presentations only waste your time and your money. Remember, the more time spent watching a show, the less time you have for observing. You would like to be able to meet with the manager of the area or group to be audited. If it's another department in the company, you would expect to meet with the department manager plus some of his or her subordinate supervisors. If the auditee is a potential vendor, you might expect the plant manager plus staff. Oftentimes all you get is the QA manager.

While this is acceptable, it also gives you a clue as to the importance the auditee places on your audit. If you only get an administrative assistant or records clerk for the opening meeting, you should probably tactfully request additional manpower.

Communication of Your Objectives

Several things should be accomplished in the opening meeting. First, the objectives of the audit should be restated. The auditee may have only vague notions of what to expect, especially if this is the first auditing experience. Usually, however, the group has been audited before and will have some idea of what to expect. The audit team leader should set the tone of the meeting by stating the objectives in a clear and diplomatic fashion. Even though these objectives have been sent to the auditee in the notification letter, it is an important human mechanism to state them in person. The audit team and auditee should also trade introductions, sometimes with a brief description of backgrounds and/or positions.

You can form important judgments during the opening meeting. Is the auditee relaxed or anxious; open or defensive? What seems to be the style of the group? Is the affected manager alone and trying to dominate the meeting? Is the staff in attendance and do they participate? Is anyone outside of the QA organization represented? These observations will prove valuable in understanding the reactions of people during interviews. They will also help when developing the tone of the report.

You must impress upon the auditee that you know their product or service line and how it affects your client's work. Reinforce the study that was done during the preparation phase by asking specific questions about the contract, or group activities in the case of an internal audit.

Communication of Areas of Concern

You might want to solicit areas of interest from the auditee. A typical response might be a desire for you to examine a newly revised control area, such as procurement or records handling. They may also wish to know how they stack up against other organizations providing a similar product or service. You should treat any expression as genuine until proven otherwise.

Conversely, you may have areas of particular concern for this audit. If your research during the preparation phase has indicated a potential

DETAILED AUDIT SCHEDULE

	Dennis Arter	Susan Clark	Leif Wilson	Gae Wong
Mon a.m.	Program	Program		
Mon p.m.	Evaluation	Evaluation		
Tue a.m.	Entrance Mtg	Entrance Mtg	Entrance Mtg	Entrance Mtg
Tue p.m.	W.O. 250270...	Proj. B-455	Proj. H-680	W.O. 250270...
Wed a.m.	W.O. 250270...	Proj. B-455	Proj. H-680	W.O. 250270...
Wed p.m.	Admin CL	Admin CL		Admin CL
Thu a.m.	Proj. B-383	W.O. 251250	Proj. H-791	Proj. H-791
Thu p.m.	Proj. B-383	W.O. 251250	Proj. H-791	Proj. H-791
Fri a.m.	Clean-up	Clean-up	Clean-up	Clean-up
Fri p.m.				

Contacts:	Work Orders	Robert C. Rubel	Bldg 210	ext. 040
	B Projects	Tom J. Campbell	Hqtrs 4th Floor	ext. 935
	H Projects	John R. Burkhart	Hqtrs 5th Floor	ext. 802
	Admin matters	Dennis Sandmeier	Bldg 19	ext. 385

35

weak area, it should be mentioned. This will help the auditee to prepare for your intense examination of that area of interest.

Settle Logistics

This is the most important part of the entrance meeting, for it affects all the effort to come. If not already accomplished before the opening meeting, the audit checklists should be presented to the auditee. It is a good idea to have at least three copies available—one to give to the senior auditee representative as a display of respect, one for you to write on during the meeting, and another for someone to copy right after the meeting.

The detailed schedule for the remainder of the audit should be developed during the entrance meeting so that the audit may proceed efficiently. A good way to accomplish this is by developing a matrix of auditors and areas, with dates and times to be filled in at the opening meeting. By discussing the information needs with the auditee, the team may be able to designate blocks of time for specified individuals. This accomplishes three important things: it forces the auditing process along, it provides for good time management for the auditee, and it encourages a constant application of auditor resources over the entire audit.

For external audits, such things as conference rooms, telephone operation, hours of operation, and lunchroom facilities can be discussed. Keep in mind that many firms require some sort of identification or security badge and often require escorts. Certain portions of the plant may require wearing safety glasses or hard hats. You must be precise in your conformance to these safety and security rules or the credibility of the entire team will suffer.

Perceptions

Most of us recognize that the world as we see it is not necessarily as it really is. A good job to one of us may be a sloppy job to another. Often, we are presented with the same set of facts as someone else. Our perception of these facts and resulting conclusions will be different depending upon our individual needs and viewpoints. People, including auditors, see things differently. As mentioned earlier, you may have developed considerable bias over time and familiarity with your surroundings. Of course, the same thing has happened to those you will be auditing. These different views may be quite honestly and stubbornly held.

Perceptions

Same Facts - Different Conclusions

You must recognize this situation and attempt to overcome it. Here are three concepts to consider if you wish to persuade your client and the audited organization that your perception of the facts is better (more useful) than their perception of those same facts:

- Present items and facts that will satisfy the needs of the audited and auditing organizations. Make a contribution. Show how the facts affect the product or service.

- Ignore or downplay mildly disturbing things. Don't nitpick. Strive to answer the "So what?" response.

- Pay attention to significant things. Chronic or persistent problems and weaknesses, along with trends, will get the attention of your audience.

Granted, these concepts have much to do with the report of the audit and the way in which you present your conclusions, but you must be aware of these needs and perceptions during the performance phase in order to gather the proper information. Additionally, you will have many opportunities to present small summaries and con- clusions throughout the audit. You should be prepared to address these perception issues from the beginning.

Understand the System

In any organization, there are two control systems: the formal one and the actual one. They will never be the same. It is the differences between the two that will vary from company to company and de- partment to department. Experience has shown that the better firms tend to minimize the gap between theory and reality. In order to measure this gap, you must understand both types of controls.

Formal Controls

The formal control system is that described to outsiders in written documents. These usually consist of organization charts, company policies, flow charts, and various manuals and procedures. The tools that you use to understand this formal system are your checklist questions. Although much of the initial examination of these formal control systems was accomplished during the preparation phase, you should further probe the key or critical control points during the performance phase. These key points usually include interfaces with other departments and groups (both internal and external), reporting methods, and even accounting controls. Be careful with the latter. As outsiders, you have a very limited need to know financial data. By combining your preparation studies and on-site data gathering, you should now have a good idea of how things are supposed to be.

Informal Controls

In addition to understanding the formal control system, you must also identify, understand, and evaluate the actual control system. Any such system may be thought of as being comprised of the four ele- ments of planning, performance, monitoring, and correction dis- cussed in Chapter 1. No matter what the activity being controlled, these elements will normally work:

- Establish responsibilities and authorities for various important parts of the activity. Who's in charge?

- Segregate important duties so that there is a division of the work effort. One person cannot do everything.

- Plan and review important actions before they're started. Develop a way for authorizing the start of work.

- Develop a means for measuring and recording information on the process or activity being controlled.

- Monitor the activity so that effective feedback may be used. Implement corrective action that will address the cause of a problem in addition to the immediate deficiency.

These are the control elements you need to examine for actual application. Because most of your knowledge will come from the discussions you have with people trying to implement the formal and informal control systems, an understanding of proper interview techniques is most valuable for successful auditing.

Interview Technique

As stated earlier, a good auditor posesses skill, training, and personal attitudes of a special nature. Part of this magical quality is the ability to conduct useful interviews of the auditee. This interview process can be broken down into six steps:[2] (1) putting the person at ease, (2) explaining your purpose, (3) finding out what they are doing, (4) analyzing what they are doing, (5) making a tentative conclusion, and (6) explaining your next step.

In each of these steps, you must deal with the human person. Remember, they possess the information you need for success!

1. *Put them at ease.* Consider yourself to be a guest in a home and grant your interviewee the respect you would give to a host. Your purpose here is to give that other person an opportunity to size you up and to lower the natural sense of anxiety. This step may range from a simple introduction and handshake to discussions about the parking lot or weather. Often, the person being interviewed is threatened by your presence and may even perceive their job to be in jeopardy if "wrong" answers are given. Unless these barriers are removed, little information will be obtained.

2. *Explain your purpose.* The natural first reaction to your presence might be, "Why me?" You must address that concern immediately. What information do you want? Why are you asking all these questions? Most people will express a desire to share information once they know why you want it. In a way, it makes them feel important and strengthens the human bond that's forming.

It is in this early stage of the interview process that a demonstration of competence is important. You should be aware of the effect your appearance has on others and dress accordingly. More important, however, is the impression created by being well organized and exhibiting a knowledge of the subject matter being discussed. You need not be an expert in the field, but you should at least be aware of the commonly used terms and associated processes. Be careful, however, to refrain from discussing explicit controls or practices that you have seen elsewhere. Such "showing off" will only damage your usefulness. In the case of an external audit, your discussion of another's proprietary methods could be grounds for legal action against you or your employer.

3. *Find out what they are doing.* During your preparation for the audit, you should have examined the formal control systems and identified areas to explore. You now continue the investigation process by asking open-ended questions: "How does the Frizzel Form get started?" "What is your first action upon receipt of a requisition?" By avoiding questions which give "yes" or "no" answers, you will get much more information. If the answers are incomplete, try, "And then what happens?"

You should also avoid statements, such as "I understand you keep the Tool Inventory Sheet." In legal circles this is called a "leading question" and is designed to elicit a specific response. The way you phrase the question leads the respondent to give you the answer they think you are expecting. If you ask this kind of question, you may not get the entire truth.

During this part of the interview process, it is helpful to get that other person to show you the forms, printouts, and memos being discussed. This not only helps you to understand the control process, it also contributes to the examination by providing concrete examples of the verbal explanations. It also tends to direct some of the natural tensions towards an inanimate piece of paper.

You have two ears and one mouth, so you should probably listen twice as long as you talk! This is certainly not the time to lecture the other person or brag about your accomplishments. If your question produces a satisfactory answer, make a notation and proceed to the next question. The necessary pause periods while you write should be as brief as possible. You should always strive to reduce the tension, and silence is usually uncomfortable. One technique often quite effective is to "write out loud" as you place information in your checklist. Also remember that this is not a trial.

You now have a bunch of marks and notes on your checklist. You have gathered a lot of information but you are not finished with the interview yet! Some important (and often forgotten) steps follow.

4. *Analyze what they are doing.* Once you have heard the words, you must analyze what those words mean. If you are familiar with the control process being discussed, your job here becomes somewhat easier. When there is a logical break in the questioning, rephrase the answers to improve the chance that you understand. "Let me see if I have that straight; first you receive and log . . . ." Such "thinking out loud" forces you to put the facts in perspective and in some sort of logical arrangement.

Occasionally you will receive an answer which is incomplete or clearly at variance with the requirements of the formal control system. Attempt to resolve the issue by looking for areas of agreement and defer the area of disagreement for later. Give the other person the opportunity to save face—the omission or lack of control may not have been important after all, or it may have been an inadvertent error. It is useful to stress supporting or contributing statements and assure yourself that you are not nitpicking.

5. *Make a tentative conclusion.* It is now time to state your conclusions. This concept of *no secrets* is sometimes hard to practice; we don't want to tell someone that they are doing something wrong. This is why employee performance reports are often deferred or meaningless. But you are obligated to tell the interviewee what you think. Your final report will benefit as well.

If your initial analysis indicates that all is well, it is appropriate to say, "The system as I understand it appears to be as follows . . ., and that meets the requirements of . . . ." Let that other person know that he or she is doing something good. They will continue to perform well with such recognition by an outsider.

If there is a deficiency, give them an opportunity to produce additional factual evidence to show that you have made an error. The discussion should be unemotional and professional. Do not convey glee at having found a deficiency or anger at what seems to be an evasive answer. Remember that you will have the last word in the report. You know it and they know it. A problem cannot be solved by taking a stand or playing win/lose. If doubt remains at the end of the discussion, then say so. Do not say, "You haven't convinced me of . . ."; rather say, "There still seems to me to be an opening . . . perhaps I'll understand it better when I review the data."

By practicing this philosophy of no secrets, any errors you may have made will be corrected early in this interview phase rather than at a formal closing meeting or after the report is issued. Additionally, you have provided vital feedback to the employee; good performance will continue and poor performance will be corrected. Everyone wins!

6. *Explain your next step.* The final step of the interview process is to conclude the discussions and let that other person know what's next. If you feel that you have about all the information you can get from them, then state, "Thank you for your help. I don't believe we'll need to get back with you again." Whew! They can now go back to work and once more be productive employees. If all your questions have not been answered, you may wish to make another appointment. If you intend to check out additional records as a result of the interview, then this too should be stated. It is important to remember that people want to know: (1) how they did in the interview, and (2) whether they are finished.

The keys to a good interview are: (1) rigorous preparation, and (2) a genuine desire to know and understand the other person's viewpoint. You must remember that these are other human beings and not printed circuits that you are dealing with. They have the advantage of having a valuable commodity (information) which you desire. If you act like a guest in their home and stick to the principle of *no secrets*, your interview will be a success.

Verify the System

The verification process normally takes most of the time and effort in the performance phase of the audit. Verification is the collection and analysis of facts upon which findings will be made and opinions will be rendered. We have read what has been written. We have listened to what has been said. It's time to smell the factory.

In Chapter 3 you were introduced to several sources of facts. Recall that these are: physical examination, confirmation, observation, documentation, interviews, and comparisons and relationships. Also remember that the two fundamental questions to be answered by an audit are: (1) Is the control system implemented? (2) Is the control system working?

The activities of audit preparation and understanding the control systems facilitate answering these questions; however, they provide no tangible proof. Your client and the auditees will require such proof if your conclusions are to be credible. The best way to obtain this proof is by examination of the product, which is the output of the organization you are auditing.

In a factory, the product is usually readily identifiable—valves, motors, relays, doors. If you are not sure of all the specific products being made, wander over to the shipping dock and see what is being put on the truck. Internally, the product is usually some action performed for another group. Regardless of the kind of product, you must find a way to tie your audit conclusions back to that which is tangible. The easiest way to accomplish this tie is through the three verification tools of tracing, sampling, and corroboration.

Tracing

Tracing is a commonly used means of collecting evidence during the audit. It can involve almost every facet of the system being examined and will result in a well-defined picture of the actual practices. To *trace* means to follow the progress of something as it is processed. The item being traced may be tangible, like a fabricated tank, or intangible, like information. You may even wish to develop your own flowchart of the product or process being examined, based upon the written procedures you studied earlier. In the manufacturing industries, many firms use "travelers" for their fabrication and assembly control. They can be used as road maps for your tracing activities. Tracing is extremely useful where intangible activities, such as design, procurement or data processing, are being audited.

The mechanics of tracing are relatively simple:

- Start either at the beginning or the end of the process

- Choose one or more transactions

- Follow the path of the transaction backward or forward through the process

Verification by tracing rests upon the assumption that the path taken fairly represents the actual functioning of the process. Therefore, you must be careful while being led through the maze by the auditee. Often, you may get a clearer picture of the controls being practiced by choosing which transactions to trace ahead of time. Here again, it is important to select those transactions which are meaningful to the quality of the product or service being produced by the audited organization.

Sampling

Obviously, you or your team leader will choose what evidence to collect, how much time to spend collecting it, and what not to collect. It is often not practical to collect evidence for each question on your checklists. You are in the position of trying to find the truth in a limited amount of time and are thus left with decisions on how much evidence to collect. A powerful tool for making this decision is sampling. That power arises from several considerations.

- The sample size may be determined in advance.

- The sample result may be compared with 100% examination.

- The result is unbiased, objective, defensible, and repeatable by anyone.

- Sampling conserves time.

However, before you go out and start pulling jeans pockets off the line, four questions must be answered:

1. What is to be sampled?

2. What will the results mean?

3. How is the sample to be taken?

4. How much is to be sampled?

1. *What is to be sampled?* Whether you are limited by someone else or by your own actions is irrelevant because the result is the same. You are unable to verify everything. Thus, the answer to the question is simply, the critical items. Avoid the vast mass of things which are trivial or less important. Here are some guidelines for determining the critical few:

- Checklist preparation will reveal major items and areas.

- Interviews should reveal areas that are important in the eyes of the auditee.

- Interfaces, where responsibility passes from one organization to another, are often the source of mistakes and imperfection.

- Overloaded or stressed activities, where the resources are being strained, should be examined.

- Work in a completely different area or process, where there is a learning curve of new or different assignments, should be probed.

- Sometimes the completely routine activities have a long history of being able to hide inefficiencies. These should be probed occasionally.

The guidelines are listed in order of importance. Remember, however, that much depends upon the experience of the auditors and the situation at hand.

2. *What will the results mean?* You want to be pretty sure that your conclusions are right. Obviously you would like to be certain but you must settle for something less. In general, your results should have 90 to 95 percent assurance that you are correct. The statistical people call this a *95 percent confidence factor.* As we shall soon see, this may be a difficult level to attain.

3. *How to sample?* The mechanics of how to sample are quite simple: Draw a random sample from the population. That way, each and every item in the pile has an equal chance of selection. To illustrate, you have decided that you are going to verify that vendors have up-to-date drawings and specifications, because this is a key control interface. You have also decided that a certain component is critical.

The random selection is made by pulling purchase orders, drawings, or specifications from the purchasing file. These documents may be filed serially, monthly, or in some other sequence. Using a random number table, you choose some number of items from the sequence. If the method of evidence you have chosen is confirmation, you would then call the vendor and ask for purchase order requirements, drawing revision numbers, or whatever information bit you are seeking to verify. You compare the auditee's file with the vendor information and note the results on your checklist work paper.

4. *How much to sample?* The question of how much to sample or how many items to verify depends on two things: How sure do you want to be that your conclusion is correct (we have at least indicated that you should want to be 90 to 95 percent certain), and how many occurrences are there?

To illustrate: If the pile (population) is the purchase order file and it contains 1,000 purchase orders, you would reasonably believe that, if there were a large number of orders with a deficiency in that pile (say 200), a fairly small sample would quickly show that a problem existed. Whereas, if the number of deficiencies in the pile were small (say 50), you would have to sample many more documents before you could draw a conclusion. And your belief would be correct. For the case illustrated, you would need to take 13 samples from the "200-bad" pile to achieve a 95 percent confidence in your conclusion. However, the "50-bad" pile would need 55 samples for the same conclusion! You can see that as the number of discrepancies becomes less, the sample size must get bigger if you are to have the same degree of confidence. The major difficulty in choosing how much to sample is that you do not know how many errors may exist in the first place.

In many audit reports, findings such as the following are common: "Three folders revealed no signature," or "Five drawings were reviewed and two had incorrect revision numbers." Zero signatures in a sample of three may mean that no folders are ever signed. In the case of two out of five, the true state may lie anywhere between 8 percent and 92 percent having wrong revisions—not a precise and unambiguous answer. As a practical matter, samples of 30 to 100 are sufficiently precise for most audits. In addition to the value of statistical rigor, these can serve an extremely useful psychological function. Two out of five may well be perceived as "nit-picking," especially where the wrong revision number on those particular drawings is not a critical characteristic.

If a larger sample, say 50, is used, the finding may state: "A sample of 50 drawings was reviewed and 18 had incorrect revision numbers." This may allow you to make a rather precise statement that at least one third of the drawings in the system have incorrect revision numbers. You could make a precise confidence statement like, "There is a 95 percent confidence that wrong revision numbers occur in 34 to 38 percent of the drawings." However, this kind of precision is not recommended in an audit report for the simple reason that most management people won't really understand it. The first statement should have the desired effect. You have gone beyond what is mildly disturbing and highlighted something really significant.

Corroboration

The third major verification method is corroboration, which is the support of a "fact" by other independent evidence. Corroboration is generally accomplished by two auditors verifying the "facts" from two or more sources. For example, in a data processing audit, one auditor may examine code module control and conclude that there is a high probability that source code revisions are not controlled. Another auditor examining code testing may conclude that not all major changes are validated. The two pieces of evidence would support the conclusion that there is lack of source code change control. Corroboration may also be obtained from separate records; for example, the inspection log may record 100 parts inspected and the production log may record 120 parts shipped. Because perceptions vary, a statement made during an interview is not a fact until it is corroborated by someone else or verified by a document.

Recommendations

Those who have had experience in auditing or who have received audit reports, may have noted a significant departure from conventional practice, in that the term *recommendations* has yet to be used.

When the audit group starts to provide solutions to another organization's management control problems, the inevitable result is a decrease in the quality of the product or service. There are several reasons for this:

Malicious Compliance

The receiving organization often does not know what you really mean in a suggestion and may be angry at you for making it in the first place. So they do an obviously stupid thing just to show you how far off base you are. Remember, the quickest way to get your boss in trouble is to do exactly what he or she says. Then you can always say, "I did just what you told me to do."

Inadequate Knowledge

Problems, by their very nature, are often difficult to solve. At times, this may require a very extensive analysis or an in-depth investigation. In the limited time for an audit, the team cannot always devote the resources necessary to find the true underlying cause(s) to a difficult problem, so the solution is inadequate.

Perceived Bias

You may be tempted to suggest or recommend a solution based upon your prior experience in a similar situation. But because your solution was "not invented here" it becomes suspect and you stand a chance of being accused of bias.

Ownership of Quality

If you allow yourself to recommend, suggest, or direct the necessary corrective action, then you have assumed at least partial ownership of the problem, with little or no resources to correct it. This is not an ideal position to be in. You have become a crutch for the management of the organization on the receiving end of the recommendation. Ownership of the quality of the product or service is no longer clearly defined; you have taken some of that ownership away. And when you take away ownership, you remove responsibility and accountability.

This concept of the ownership of quality is most important to success. Managers are paid good money to provide quality products and services and must be held accountable for the resulting work. The job of an auditor is to provide analyzed information—to be another set of eyes and ears for managers. You must find and analyze the true impediments to quality and then let affected managers and supervisors correct those problems. Does this mean that the auditors should just point out problems and then walk away? Of course not. But you must not impose your methods and approaches on the audited group. If asked, then you should certainly offer the benefit of your experience in having seen good and not-so-good methods.

If your firm requires that recommendations be placed in an audit report, then you should phrase them so that meaningful frameworks are provided without specific detail. In reality, recommendations are seldom optional. There is a great deal of pressure to do precisely what the auditor says, whether it contributes to quality or makes things worse. You should be aware of this reaction in your discussions with the auditee. Carefully phrase your observations as solicited advice rather than required actions. Even though the report has yet to be issued, some of your utterances may become edict.

Findings and Observations

Most audit programs will use the terms *finding* and *observation* when presenting the unsatisfactory conclusions of the audit.[3] It should be recognized that the definitions of these two words are not universal from company to company, but,in general, they both address negative things. Seldom is a *finding* presented as a positive (or neutral) conclusion. Also, an *observation* is usually less severe than a *finding*.

A *finding* is a statement of fact regarding noncompliance with established policy, procedures, instructions, drawings, or other applicable documents. A *finding* is something that can lead to, or has resulted in, a condition adverse to quality. It is a conclusion supported by enough evidence to convince the auditee that you have indeed found a problem that needs to be investigated and corrected. Or, put another way, a promise has not been kept.

An *observation* is a detected program weakness, which, if not corrected, will result in a degradation of product or service quality. *Observations* may be thought of as precursors to *findings*. Note that *observations* do not include serious or significant noncompliances; if they did then they would be *findings*. They should be used to alert the auditee of your concerns and potential areas of trouble.

Team Meetings

The final step in the performance phase is the team meeting. Last is definitely not least! It is sound practice to leave about 30 minutes at the end of each day (or the beginning of the next day) for the team to meet. These sessions should be informally structured, but include three areas:

- Sharing of facts, tentative conclusions, and problems.

- Replanning for the next day's activities. This is sort of a repeat of the preparation phase.

- Developing the audit report.

The sharing of facts and tentative conclusions enriches the audit process. Talking over what has been learned during the day's investigation allows for team corroboration of facts and possible areas for deeper investigation. Discussions should also include the perceptions drawn during the interview process. Is there a thread of activity that is done extremely well or very poorly? Does the evidence gathered by each individual auditor point to a more general conclusion about the controls used and their implementation? The questions and discussions should bring into sharper focus tentative *findings* and *observations*. Facts collected during the day should be organized and sorted in order to support your conclusions, both positive and negative. Where pieces of evidence are either insufficient or completely missing, you can then make plans to fill in these gaps.

The result from this sharing could be replanning or redirection of the audit. Keep in mind, however, that you are obligated to stick to the original purpose and scope. Based on information now available, the following issues can be addressed:

- Are the results of the interviews and evidence-gathering sufficient to reach a conclusion?

- Should there be additional interviews, additional checklist questions, or additional evidence?

- Are there administrative problems to be resolved with the audited organization or the audit team?

- Does the audit seem to be accomplishing its objectives?

Tentative Conclusions

As you conduct interviews and gather data, you will reach conclusions about the performance of the audited organization in the specific area you are pursuing. You should write these down in draft form. They may be either good or bad practices which are candidates for the final report. At the team meeting, these draft statements may be polished, consolidated with others, or discarded. In any event, they are extremely useful for beginning the reporting phase.

Brief the Auditee

You can now see that effective team meetings are an important key to successful audits. Likewise, daily briefings with the auditee will enhance the quality of your audit. If a goal of improved performance is to be attained, it is important that there be *NO SURPRISES* to the auditee. This communication with the auditee can best be accomplished by a short and informal briefing of about 10 minutes at the end of each day with someone from the audited group. Topics to be discussed include:

- Checklist areas completed

- Checklist areas to be examined tomorrow

- Any areas of concern

- Any problems experienced

If you've uncovered something out of wack, it is certainly not necessary (or desirable) to present potential *findings* or *observations* yet. Rather, explain to the representative that these are "potential problem areas" or "areas of concern" at this stage of the audit. You know that as soon as this meeting is finished, the representative will brief his or her manager. They will try to make that problem go away. The audited organization becomes motivated to help you by providing additional facts to verify or refute your concerns. If you were wrong because of incorrect or insufficient information, the item is prevented from appearing in the final report. If they truly do have a problem, the additional digging has helped to reinforce the fact. Either way, both parties win.

Onward

The next phase of the audit process is the reporting phase; although you may have noticed that much of the discussion in this chapter has concerned itself with the report. This is because there is no sharp boundary line between the two phases. The report is being proposed, modified, rejected, and rebuilt by the entire team both individually and jointly, as the audit progresses. You must keep it in mind throughout the performance of the audit. Starting the report on the first day of data gathering has at least four merits:

1. It helps structure the audit by forcing you to develop hypotheses early.

2. The writing of tentative conclusions, findings, and observations forces precision in the audit process.

3. The problem of sorting, digesting, and reviewing a large mass of material before the exit meeting deadline is reduced.

4. Factual errors, perceptual errors, and other distortions are reduced.

Chapter 5 contains more detailed discussion on specific aspects of your report.

Footnotes

[1]Even a short process audit (surveillance) should have a brief entrance meeting. Often, this is just a notification to the shift supervisor that you will be in the area performing an audit for the next 30 minutes.

[2]Original concept developed by Frank X. Brown, *The Practice and Process of Auditing,* 1979, Westinghouse Electric Corporation.

[3]The ASQC's Q-1 Standard uses the term *observation* for any specific audit conclusion, good or bad, yet uses the term *finding* when discussing corrective action. Their A3 standard on Quality Systems Terminology uses the term *finding* in conjunction with something requiring corrective action. The General Accounting Office publishes reports wherein significant deficiencies and problems are referred to as *findings*. The Comptroller General of the United States has published standards for government audits, requiring copies of the audit report to go to those responsible for action on audit *findings,* again, implying something negative. The Institute of Internal Auditors, in their *Standards for the Professional Practice of Internal Auditing,* states that action should be taken on reported audit *findings.* They use the term *audit conclusions* in a generic fashion with neither positive nor negative connotation. The nuclear standard ANSI/ASME NQA-1 uses the term audit *finding* to denote an adverse condition requiring corrective action. Unfortunately, the author has been able to locate but one standard which specifically defines the term *finding.* The "Generic Requirements for Auditing Nuclear Materials Safeguards Systems (ANSI N15.38-1982)," identifies a *finding* as a condition at variance with a requirement.

CHAPTER 5

REPORTING

The Report Is Your Product

The audit report is your final *PRODUCT*. All of the sights, sounds, smells, observations, scraps of paper, tensions, and anxieties are finally reduced into something for others to read. When everything is closed out, the only evidence of your presence is the report! It is your means of communicating information to others. As such, it should have certain characteristics in order to be successful.

Verifiability

Your reports should be verifiable. The reader may not always be able to verify them personally, since we cannot track down the evidence for every piece of history known. But if you use generally accepted names for things, like *foot, yard, milling machine,* and so on, there is relatively little danger of your message being misunderstood. When you refer back to specific items or locations at the audit site, whether it be internal or external, the perception of verifiability is enhanced. Of course, one of the main purposes of a structured checklist is to record verification information. However, putting checklist-like detail in the report makes it too cumbersome and unreadable. Your completed checklist should be kept in the files as backup.

> "I know you believe you understand what you think I said, but I am not sure you realize that what you heard is not what I meant."

Even though it appears (especially to the new auditor) as if everybody seems to be quarreling with everybody else, we still trust information from others. We ask street directions of total strangers. We follow directions on soup cans without being suspicious of the people who wrote those directions. We read books about science, space travel, the history of party dresses, and even auditing, and we assume that the author is trying hard to tell the true story. Most of the time, we are safe in our assumptions. Despite the talk of media bias, we have an enormous amount of reliable information available. Deliberate misinformation is still more the exception than the rule. The reader wants to believe your report because of basic human desires. With simple, clear, and direct language, you can reinforce that desire.

Inferences

An inference is a statement about the unknown made on the basis of the known. You may infer lack of control over donut size from your examination of the blending and mixing sheets. You may infer lack of actual control from the fact that two of five, or six of 24, donuts pulled from the line were too small. In fact, an audit requires that you make inferences such as these. Thus, the question is not, "Should you make inferences?" but rather, "Are you aware of the inferences you make?" The technique of gathering and analyzing facts will allow you to present these inferences in an understandable and logical fashion. Anyone may retrace your path and should make the same inference. But since this is unlikely to happen, you must take the approach that a reasonable person, presented with the same facts you have seen, will draw conclusions similar to yours. Their inferences will match yours.

As a practical matter, most people will need more convincing (stronger facts and more of them) if the inference does not support a previously held conviction. This is not surprising. Any student of debate knows that it is quite difficult to change a long-held perception, even if that perception is wrong.

Judgments

Judgments are expressions of approval or disapproval. Like inferences, they cannot be avoided, so you must be aware of the judgments used in your report. The most important part of the entire report, the summary section, is basically one big judgment.

A statement such as, "Your design control system meets the requirements of MIL-Q-9858A," is a judgment. "Welding is a special process," is also a judgment. Because they have a relatively broad basis of understanding, they will normally be accepted as fact, provided the underlying standards or definitions do not change. As with inferences, those judgments supporting a previously held belief will be accepted quickly; whereas, judgments contrary to those beliefs will be resisted. If your judgments are of an adverse nature, they may be subject to distortion on the receiving end unless you take great pains to make them as clear and understandable as possible.

Summary Section

The credibility and acceptance of your report is substantially improved when it includes an assessment of overall performance. "How well are we doing?" is a fair question, and some statement of analysis will go far in meeting the needs of your client. Remember, you're getting paid to answer the two basic questions of whether the control systems are in place and if they work. The summary is therefore the most important part of the entire report. Despite opinions to the contrary, you should never be placed in the position where you must have a certain number of *findings* in an audit report. Such a quota system is reflective of past practices where audits only reported bad things. It's OK to state that things are working well, like they should be, and that only a few minor problems exist.

Usually, a one-paragraph general discussion of the overall analysis of the control areas examined is sufficient. Because your readers are managers, the words should be phrased in management terms. This should be followed by a one- to two-sentence presentation of each of the really important *findings,* if there are any. When you have problems to report, this combination of summary and highlighted *findings* will get the attention of senior management, in your own (or client) organization as well as the auditee's. If well prepared, it should stimulate interest in hearing about the details. It should lead to a desire to do something about any problems perceived by the audit team.

A summary will balance out the (by definition) negative tone of any *findings* and *observations.* As humans, we respond much better to criticism when we are told that the overall program is working, but that there are a few areas in need of correction. The team will be recognized as competent and unbiased if the summary presents a professional, honest, and straightforward picture.

Sometimes, during the course of an audit, you will come across a group performing exceptionally well. Is this a judgment? You bet it is! Don't, however, water down your report by calling everything exceptional. Remember that people and groups are expected to perform well in our capitalistic system, that's why we pay them large sums of money. However, you should acknowledge those cases where the auditee is performing above and beyond the call of duty. Do this by devoting a separate paragraph to a description of the situation and how it affects the quality of the product or service under examination. Call this an *exemplary practice* if you wish and place it right after the summary section.

Findings

The preparation of the report continues with the development of any *findings* and/or *observations* proposed by the various members of the team during the data gathering stage. First, collect and discuss all of the issues, including the evidence that supports each of them. Remember that a *finding* is a condition adverse to quality. If not corrected, the quality of the goods and services will continue to suffer. Remember too that the main objective of auditing is to improve the performance of the area or activity being examined. This requires that *findings* be stated in terms that will arouse management interest and convince them that there are serious problems which need to be investigated and corrected.

Generic Issues

Each *finding* must be a clear, concise statement of a generic problem, one that relates to a whole group, class, or activity. Individual nonconformances, such as, "Drawing 12345, being used for the concrete pour of Highway 697, was an obsolete revision," are not *findings*. In this case, the corrective action taken by the contractor will probably be limited to replacing that drawing by the current revision. No attempt to find out why the obsolete issue was being used on that job will be made, let alone any effort to try to write a blueprint library control procedure, train personnel, or take other action on the underlying cause of this specific problem.

If there are a number of examples of incorrect blueprint revisions in use, there is indeed a generic problem. But you still don't have a very strong case and haven't convinced management that a true problem exists. You need to show how similar problems fit into the picture. For example, the team members may have prepared draft *findings* such as:

- Out of date blueprints were being used at seven milepost work areas.

- The blueprint control register was last revised on March 6th, which is three months past the date required by Engineering Procedure 7.5.

- Red-lined drawings were noted in the guardrail fabrication shop, without evidence of approval authority. This is in violation of Engineering Procedure 3.6.

- Field inspection change notices were not referenced on 12 blueprints in use, as required by Construction Order 6–2.

All of these should be consolidated into one truly generic *finding*, such as: *"WORK INSTRUCTION DOCUMENTS ARE NOT EFFECTIVELY CONTROLLED."*

This *finding* should be followed by a brief restatement of the particular control element that is in need of attention—the requirement for controlling documents in this example—and then a listing of the individual facts which show the basis for the statement.[1] It is usually better to number each of the facts so that they may stand alone. These discussion points now show how the evidence logically leads to the *finding*. A reasonable person (the reader) seeing those facts will draw the same conclusion that you have drawn.

So What?

Findings should be tied to actual adverse conditions which affect the product or service that is being produced by the auditee. For example: The lack of documented procedures for returned material led to being unable to locate six out of 30 circuit boards. This leads to the bigger question: "Are those six mixed with conforming ones?" That type of presentation is difficult for an auditee to ignore. Similarly, *observations* should be tied to areas where corrections could result in improved performance or results. They should generate some tangible benefit to the auditee.

Often, the first response of the auditee to the suggestion of a problem will be "So what?" You must convince the reader that a serious condition exists and that it is affecting the operation of the company. Products and services are suffering as a result of this condition. You must aim for those management "hot buttons," the truly important elements of operation. High on most managers' hit parade is the station WII-FM (What's In It For Me). This means cost, schedule, productivity, and other such real-world motivators. If you can show how your *finding* affects these driving forces, you will achieve the results of improved performance. You have appealed to management and have provided them with a means of improving. Who can resist such a tempting item?

Six or Less

To be most effective in obtaining a good response, audit reports should generally be limited to six or fewer *findings* and/or *observations*. This stems from the Pareto principle, named after an Italian economist who formulated several laws about income distribution in the early 1900s. The major use of the principle today is in various types of analyses, because characteristics we seek are not uniformly distributed. Instead, a small percentage of certain characteristics will account for a high percentage of certain problems. The importance of distinguishing the vital few from the trivial many can be seen in almost any situation.[2] In our case, this can be translated to mean that the vital few problems will make the major contribution to lack of quality in most organizations. In addition, we humans tend to overload when presented with too many problems simultaneously. As a result, none get the attention they truly deserve. Management can effectively address and resolve five problems; they cannot address 50.

Exit Interview

The exit interview is the first formal opportunity for the audit team to present its report to the management of the audited activity. Typically, the investigative part of the audit is concluded some time on the morning of the final day. The exit interview is then scheduled for some time in the afternoon, and the audit team is left with about two to four hours to prepare something for the exit interview. If you have practiced the principle of *no secrets,* held daily caucuses, and kept the auditee apprised of your progress and any concerns, this two-hour period is adequate time to rough out something on paper to present to the auditee.

The exit interview should follow the format of the written formal report. It should be a preview of coming attractions. Even the small surveillance (process audit) should conclude with a brief summary of the results presented to the area supervisor.

The main purposes of the exit meeting are to:

- Present the summary

- Present any *findings, observations,* and/or exemplary practices

- Allow for corrections and explanations

- Explain the followup and response process if problems were identified

While the lead auditor is responsible for conducting the presentation, the entire audit team has generated the words. As lead auditor, you should start off with a recap of the audit scope and purpose and then get right into the summary. The best way to do this is in the form of a personal conversation between you, representing the audit team, and the senior manager present, representing the auditee. Look that person in the eye as you present the overall conclusions. Make them feel that the subject matter is important and that they are important. You should then present the details of any *findings* or *observations*. At this point, it is appropriate to pass out copies of the draft *findings/observations,* which are handwritten and assembled one to a page. Do not read the words out loud; rather, give them credit for being able to read by themselves. Explain the items in a conversational manner as briefly as you can, but remember that their listening abilities are diminished as they read the paper in front of them.

Disagreement

As a team member, you may disagree with the summary or some of the *findings*. Nonetheless, you had your chance in the team caucuses. The conclusions generated in these team meetings are now consensus statements. This is no time for arguments among the team members. If you were unable to convince the rest of the team of the merits of your viewpoint during the team meeting, you certainly will not be able to convince the auditee during a brief and formal exit meeting.

In preparation for the exit meeting, you should keep in mind that the facts and conclusions of the draft audit report must not be changed in the final report—except, of course, to correct any errors that are brought out in the exit meeting discussion or in subsequent reinvestigation. If you have any concerns to raise, put them in the draft report and discuss them in the exit meeting. Failure to do so, particularly if your facts are wrong, casts doubt on the entire audit program. There have been numerous cases in which the audit team lost all ground that might have been gained, because the auditee claimed they were "sandbagged" and refuted one minor fact.

Attendance

The exit interview presentation should be made to the responsible managers of the activities audited. Attendance by the quality manager alone is unsatisfactory, in that he or she may become a filter in the communication of your report to upper management. The conclusions and any *findings* or *observations* may become subject to distortion. Additionally, the owner of any problem should have an opportunity to participate in the discussion.

On the other hand, attendance by several layers of management will most probably lead to argument. It is human nature to want to defend one's position in front of the boss, even if we know that position to be wrong. So a supervisor is obligated to argue an audit *finding* in his or her area if the director is present. Also, if they are at your meeting, they may well be away from more productive work. You can limit this arguing and unproductive time by requesting attendance of just department heads.

Consider Their Viewpoint

In preparing for the exit interview, it is worthwhile to put yourself in the auditee's position and see things from that viewpoint. Remember that your objective is to change things for the better (or at least encourage the continuance of good practices). The art of the exit interview lies in persuading the auditee that your conclusions represent the true state of things. If problems were uncovered, then the consequences are serious and something can and should be done about them. It is a tough and demanding challenge for the team leader. Once finished, your whole team is exhausted, both physically and mentally. The team should promptly leave the area and disperse.

Formal Report

The formal report is the final and complete documentation of the audit. It must stand alone, in that a reasonably knowledgeable layman should be able to understand it without asking a series of questions. It should be issued within a reasonable time period after the exit meeting. Remember, for each day that the report is held up in your shop, its importance diminishes with the auditee. A common practice is to strive for issuance of the formal report within two weeks of the

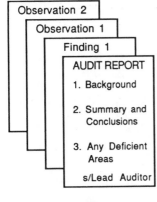

Observation 2
Observation 1
Finding 1

AUDIT REPORT

1. Background

2. Summary and
   Conclusions

3. Any Deficient
   Areas

s/Lead Auditor

The Audit Report
and Details are
Prepared by the
Audit Team

Date
To: Auditee
Fr: Client
Subj: Audit of ...

Brief Background

Executive Summary
of Results

Request for
Corrective Action

The Client (Audit Mgr)
Reviews the package
and then attaches a
Cover Letter

Auditee

Auditee receives
the Package and
Responds if Req'd

exit meeting. This can be easily accomplished if the practice of writing the report as you proceed through the audit is observed.

The report should start by presenting the necessary background information. Usually contained in a paragraph called *Introduction* or *Background,* the traditional who, what, when, where, why, and how things are presented. Keep this introductory paragraph brief or you will lose your audience within the first ten seconds.

The *Summary* or *Conclusions* paragraph should come next. As was just stated, this is the most important section of the report. But again, it must be kept brief, clear, and concise if you are to retain your audience. If any adverse conditions were identified, they should be summarized next in the second paragraph of this section. Finally, any exemplary practices are identified last.

The second sheet of the report is often a list of the people you contacted during the course of the audit. Although this level of detail is optional, it adds to the veracity of the report by showing that you talked to a broad spectrum of individuals. If any *findings* or *observations* are identified, these should appear next, normally one to a page. The report must be dated and then signed by the team leader and may also be signed by the individual team members.

Cover Memo

The most common method of transmitting the formal report is to attach it to a cover letter/memo issued by the client or other responsible manager or contract administrator. This accomplishes two important objectives: (1) it adds credibility and importance to the whole concept by the fact that the report originates from a senior individual, and (2) the issuing manager owns a portion of the report, even if you drafted the cover letter. Such ownership encourages reading of the report and establishes responsibility for poor reports.

This is not to imply that your client should be in the position of approving your team's audit report. The client has not been there and "smelled the roses" and should not be asked to report on the aroma. The report is yours alone. However, your client (typically the QA manager) is responsible for the adequacy and quality of your product. This can be accomplished through the normal supervisory review process without compromising your independence and integrity. Often, you may be requested to draft the cover memo or letter for the client's signature. The same concern with clear and effective communication applies equally or more so to this cover document, as it is the first formal sheet of paper the auditee will see.

If any problems were identified, the cover letter/memo should request a written response to all *findings* within a stated time. Practice varies with regard to responses to *observations*. Some organizations take the position that, if they are important enough to go in the audit report, a response should be required. Others believe that *observations* should be nonthreatening "freebies" and no response should be required. Your own organization's practices should apply or the lead auditor should decide what to do on a case-by-case basis. All requests for response should ask for a schedule for establishing and implementing corrective action, as well as for a description of the actions taken or planned. Thirty days from receipt of the report is not an unreasonable time period for putting together this kind of information.

Wrap Up

In this section, we considered the audit report your *PRODUCT*. It is the only permanent feature of all the work and effort that goes into an audit. It is important that the report be written as the audit progresses, not in a rush at the end.

The most important part of the audit report is the summary. This "bottom line" gives management of all organizations (auditor, auditee, and client) an analysis of the health of the examined activity from the audit team's perspective. Any problems identified through the audit must be presented so that management will take action on them. This requires that any *findings* or *observations* address the truly important issues and be presented in a fashion that will lead the reader to draw the same conclusions as the audit team.

The exit meeting is the first formal presentation of the audit results, although, the auditee should have a pretty good idea of those results if the daily briefings have been taking place. Following the exit meeting, the formal report is issued, usually under the cover of a forwarding letter or memo by the responsible manager or the contract administrator.

Footnotes

[1]An example of this format can be found in Appendix 1.

[2]This phrase, "the vital few from the trivial many," is often attributed to J. M. Juran. See *Quality Control Handbook,* 3rd edition, J. M. Juran, ed., p. 2–16, for a discussion on its origin and use.

CHAPTER 6
CLOSURE

Closure Phase

The closure phase of the audit includes the activities which follow the issuance of the formal report. These may be classified as:

- Evaluation of Response

- Audit Closeout

- Documentation

Because these items are intimately connected with the notion of *corrective action,* it is appropriate to begin with a discussion of the principles behind correcting problems.

Corrective Action

Planning and control are basic management activities, which are common to all business and government operations. The goals of management include safety, quality, cost, reliability, usefulness, and scheduling, among others. Various policies, procedures, instructions and other forms of directing are used to achieve these goals. Control is the process of monitoring those plans and identifying significant deviations from them.[1] It involves establishing a set of standards and measuring performance to those standards. Monitoring methods include inspection, test, surveillance, and, of course, auditing. Analysis of performance indicators is management's means of determining that there is a problem. Feedback is then used to make corrections so that goals can be achieved.

The principle of corrective action is that conditions adverse to quality must be promptly identified and corrected. For significant conditions adverse to quality, the cause must be determined and steps taken to preclude repetition, including the reporting of these actions to management. This latter portion of the corrective action process is often the most difficult to implement, in that true causes of problems are seldom easy to identify. Additionally, this is one of the main reasons for the lack of acceptance of quality assurance methods by many managers—it's against human nature to want to identify one's own problems before the boss. This implies that the affected supervisor has failed and, in American management circles, success, not failure, is rewarded. But without an effective and objective corrective action program, the quality of all operations will suffer greatly.

Fundamental Components of Corrective Action

Any corrective action program has three fundamental components: (1) to find problems, (2) to fix problems, and (3) to correct the causes of problems.

These three basic steps are included in the teachings of the QA masters, like Feigenbaum, Juran, and Deming, and in every published QA standard.

The audit program, along with other forms of monitoring like inspection and surveillance, will address the first step—finding problems. But as was discussed in the chapter on reporting (Chapter 5), judgments must be made and there will always be cause for different interpretations on the severity of the reported problem. This is expected and addressed in the way *findings* are presented in the audit report.

When addressing the solutions to problems, it is important that immediate correction of the specific reported deficiency not be confused with action taken to correct the cause of the problem and prevent its recurrence.[2] The function of a corrective action program is to analyze and remove these impediments to quality, safety, reliability, productivity, etc. It must be a serious and continuous process.

Response to the Audit Report

After the audit report is issued, a response is requested from the auditee if any adverse conclusions, *findings* or *observations*, are presented. As stated earlier, 30 days from receipt of the audit report is the typical turnaround time for this response. Although solicited in the exit meeting, you probably will not receive a substantive response in that period of high stress. Senior managers want to think it over before they make any significant commitments to change. This is normal and to be expected.

It is usually the team leader's responsibility to keep track of the responses to an audit report if the audit has revealed one or more deficient items. If a response is not received by the requested date, someone from your management/client team should call (or write if calls do not produce a response) to remind the audited organization of their need to positively commit to corrective action.

Adequacy of the Response

Evaluating the adequacy of the response should be a team effort if at all possible. Team members should review planned actions, in conjunction with their co-workers in affected departments, to evaluate the stated underlying causes of each *finding* and the actions planned to correct them. Personal preference should not influence the evaluation; you must decide if the planned action makes sense and has a reasonable chance for success. Your evaluation, and any comments regarding why a planned action may not be effective, should be sent to the lead auditor for inclusion in the acknowledgment to the response. If the team has scattered and it would be difficult to bring them together again, responsibility for evaluating the response may rest with the lead auditor, with input from other affected line and staff individuals.

Expected Items

A well-prepared response is straightforward and addresses each *finding* with specific corrective action steps and a schedule for completion. It is not unreasonable to expect each of the following items to be addressed in the response:

- The identification of the root cause and evaluation of the effect of the *finding* upon completed work

- A check or verification to assure that other areas or items that might have similar problems have been examined

- The actions taken to correct the problems identified in the audit report as well as those discovered during the check of other areas or items

- The identification of what action will be taken to prevent future occurrences

- Those responsible for these actions and completion date for each

Unfortunately, responses like this are seldom the case. Two major problems are often encountered: (1) the response is a defense of the status quo; and (2) the response fixes specific deficiencies without addressing the generic underlying causes.

Both problems can be minimized by good auditing and reporting. Ideally, an excellent report will result in an excellent response. Realistically, each response is an opportunity to assess your performance in auditing and report writing.

Communication Back to the Auditee

Of course you should keep the auditee informed of the status of their audit and your intentions. The concept of no secrets doesn't end after the exit meeting. If the auditee has taken the time and effort to provide a response, they deserve some sort of acknowledgment; otherwise, reaction to the next audit may be less than enthusiastic.

There are basically three options for the response evaluation. The responses include: (1) totally adequate, (2) totally inadequate, and (3) some combination of these two.

Which of these should you recommend to the team leader? In keeping with the original purpose of the audit (improved performance), the answer is straightforward. If the response addresses the issues and has a reasonable chance of success, then it should be accepted. Using this criterion, the majority of your audit responses will be acceptable.

There are, however, times when the response is judged inadequate. Once this has been decided, it may be advisable to discuss the inadequacies with the individual who signed the response. This is normally done by the team leader. Regardless of any informal discussions, the auditee should be formally notified in writing of the concerns. The client must get involved at this point. It is here that the true strength of your audit program will show. If your client managers truly believe in the value of auditing, they will back you up (and counsel you to produce better reports in the future). Working with your client and other affected managers, you should draft a letter/ memo stating why the response is deemed to be unacceptable and requesting a new response. The tone of this letter should be significantly more forceful than before.

If serious doubts about the effectiveness of corrective action plans continue and your management is unable to sway the auditee by discussion, request your client to advise the auditee that a followup visit will be performed in the near future to observe the promised corrective action. As a last resort for suppliers, your firm may wish to make effective corrective action on the *findings* a precondition for the auditee to be considered for any additional business. Such drastic action should be viewed as an indication that the audit has failed in its original purpose.

Closeout

Once the response has been analyzed and found to be acceptable, promised corrective action must be verified in some fashion. As before, the means that you use should be a team decision, with other affected line and staff people involved. Several options are available to you:

1. The response adequately describes the conditions of change and there is a reasonable chance of success. Accept the response and closeout that *finding* or *observation* immediately.

2. Some promised changes involve new or revised documents. Request that these changed documents be fowarded to you once issued. Providing the changed documents meet the requirements, the *finding* or *observation* may be closed.

3. It may be necessary for someone from your organization to perform a brief followup visit to personally verify the implementation of the promised corrective action. This person may be a member of the audit team, an affected person from another group (like the project engineer), or a third party. The visit must be limited to only the verification at hand, not a new audit area. Assuming things are satisfactory, the *findings* and *observations* may be closed.

In reality, the closeout action will probably be a combination of these three.

Periodic Status Reports

A useful technique in tracking action on audit results is to issue periodic audit status reports. These should identify:

- Each open *finding* and *observation* for each audit (internal and external)

- Any changes in target dates for actions or additional responses

- When all issues for a particular audit have been closed

Such reports can help your management assess the status of actions on audit results; and, at least for internal audits, may stimulate the audited groups to get moving.

Formal Closure

Each audit should be formally closed by letter or memo. In case of corrective actions that may be deferred for long periods, or where their effectiveness cannot be determined without a followup audit, the individual audit should be closed and followup provided by other means, such as the audit status report or commitment control system. Finally, all corrective action should be examined at the next regularly scheduled audit of that area.

Records

With good records, it should be relatively easy to convince others of the effectiveness of your audit program. You examine records in your quest for the truth; others will do likewise. In addition, good records will help when preparing for the next regularly scheduled audit.

Audit records may be classified as either official or unofficial, depending upon their use and the length of time they are kept. While practices vary throughout the nation, a good length of time to keep official records is five years. After that, the records probably won't mean much to you and most outside examiners. The following items are candidates for official records:

- Audit notification letter

- Audit plan (if a separate document)

- Blank checklists

- Audit report and cover letter

- Response from the auditee

- Closing letter

The unofficial records are kept mainly for your own use and not really used to prove anything. A good length of time to keep these records is two to three years. Some candidates for unofficial records include:

- Reference to auditor qualifications

- Audit notes

- Used checklists

- Documents obtained from auditee

- Additional correspondence

A good way to keep these records is to assemble everything from a particular audit into two folders: long-term and short-term. Set aside one file cabinet or file drawer for only these records. Then before completely closing an audit, assemble all the necessary records and place them in the proper folder. Periodically, folders may be purged to make room for new ones.

A Recap

In this chapter, we considered the activities following the reporting phase. Those activities include evaluating the auditee's response, determining the appropriate verification of the promised corrective action, keeping the auditee informed of the status of the audit, and assembling the necessary records.

The evaluation of the auditee's response is perhaps the most difficult part of the closeout action. If there is a reasonable chance of success (improved performance) then the response should be accepted.

Footnotes

[1]The terms found in MIL-STD-105D (Sampling Procedures/Inspection by Attribute) are sometimes useful in determining what is significant:

- Critical problems result in hazardous or unsafe conditions or prevent operation of the device or use of the product.

- Major problems result in specific parts failures or reduced reliability of the component.

- Minor problems are those which do not reduce usability or operation of the device.

[2]Vice Admiral Rickover of the U.S. Navy nuclear submarine fleet used to say that "problems have half-lives," meaning that they will always recur because of an ever-changing environment. Thus, it is often stated that corrective actions should reduce or minimize the chance of, rather than prevent, recurrence.

CHAPTER 7

POSTSCRIPT

You have seen how the basic monitoring methods originally developed by accountants can be used to improve any type of activity, large or small, internal or external. The keys to success are no different here than in any other business venture:

- Thorough preparation

- Rigorous performance

- Meaningful reporting

- Effective follow-up

Whether you perform audits of the major products leaving your plant, the processes used to make various items, the performance of other departments, or the actions of your suppliers, you use the same basic auditing skills. These skills are developed by formal training coupled with real-life practice. Skilled auditors are one of your company's or agency's greatest assets. They know the processes, people, and procedures. They understand internal and external customer relationships. And they possess the ability to communicate to management.

Ideally, auditors should possess a balance of emotional, mechanical, and intellectual skills. They must be able to conduct interviews, control a hostile group, convince a skeptical audience, and understand different perspectives. They must also be skilled in the mechanics of sampling, tracing, analysis, and other forms of data processing. Finally, they must be able to organize a campaign and communicate to their fellow humans. These are not easy skills to obtain. They can only be developed through study, practice, and feedback.

It is the responsibility of the manager in charge of the audit program to demand excellence and provide feedback. If one allows poor reports to be published, then eventually all reports will achieve that level of mediocrity. If the audit program does not contribute to the betterment of the firm or agency, it should not be allowed to survive. Thus, it is important to always remember that the goal of auditing is to improve the performance of the audited activity.

Skills Required of an Auditor

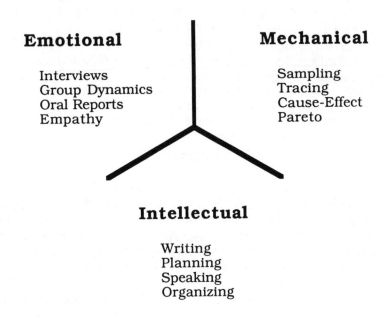

Emotional

Interviews
Group Dynamics
Oral Reports
Empathy

Mechanical

Sampling
Tracing
Cause-Effect
Pareto

Intellectual

Writing
Planning
Speaking
Organizing

This text has presented some basic concepts and theories of the quality audit process. It has also attempted to present some practical ways of implementing the theory. As the application of quality auditing becomes more established, certain methods will grow and others will die. This is to be expected. Auditing, like all the "soft" sciences, is an evolutionary process. Regardless of the changes, however, the purpose of the audit will always be to provide management with meaningful information upon which to base decisions. Through proper application, these decisions will cause performance to improve.

APPENDIX 1

INTERNAL AUDIT PROCEDURE

General

This procedure is intended to cover the implementation of the internal [company] auditing system. It does not address auditing of external suppliers, nor does it address the manner in which [company] responds to audits performed on its activities by others.

Scheduling

Internal [company] audits shall be performed in a cost-effective manner consistent with the needs of the various customers and resources available. To meet these criteria, annual audit planning shall be conducted in the first quarter after the new fiscal year. By the end of the first quarter each year, the *MANAGER, AUDITS,* shall issue an annual audit planning schedule based upon the following criteria:

1. Large Projects/Programs—These shall be identified and scheduled individually. There is no precise definition of *large;* however, factors to consider should be contract amount ($> $1M$), personnel assigned (> 20 staff), importance to some national effort, and potential risk to the company.

2. Groups of Projects—Those projects performing similar tasks for the same customer shall be identified and scheduled as a group.

3. Single Projects—Those projects not large, but not able to be classified as part of a group, shall be identified and scheduled individually. The needs of the customer shall be considered, as well as the [company] resources available for auditing. It is not intended that all projects within [company] be scheduled or even audited.

4. Department or Section—At least one audit shall be scheduled each year to examine the implementation of the [company] QA program within a department or section. This is considered to

be above and beyond the annual appraisal of QA program effectiveness required by company policy.

5. Administrative Activity—Because the following activities affect all projects and programs within the company, they shall be scheduled individually:

- Procurements

- Records management

- Document control

Other activities may be added as required.

The annual audit planning schedule shall identify these audited activities and the month in which they are scheduled for audit. No further definition (specific dates, auditors, requirements, etc.) is required or desired. The annual audit planning schedule shall be distributed to all departments and sections within the company, and to affected customers when required, by the *DIRECTOR, QUALITY ASSURANCE*. This distribution shall be controlled in accordance with the measures defined in [Procedure-601]. The annual audit planning schedule may be modified only once before a new schedule is required to be prepared and distributed.

Quarterly Schedule

Quarterly audit planning schedules shall be developed by the *MANAGER, AUDIT,* based on the annual audit planning schedule. These quarterly schedules shall contain the following information:

- Audited activity (from annual schedule)

- Start date

- Audit team leader

These quarterly schedules shall be distributed to all affected project or program managers, and others as deemed necessary, prior to the start of each quarter by the *MANAGER, AUDITS*. These schedules may be modified to suit circumstances, as long as all planned audits are performed within the affected quarter. Should any audits appearing on the annual plan be deferred during the affected quarter, the reason for such deferral shall be documented by the *DIRECTOR, QUALITY ASSURANCE.*

Audit Planning

Prior to the performance of an audit, an audit plan shall be prepared and appropriate parties shall be notified. Audit plans shall be prepared by the audit team leader and contain the following information:

- Audit title

- Audit number (sequentially by calendar year: 89–01, 89–02, etc.)

- Scope

- Requirements (audit base)

- Audit personnel

- Activities to be audited

- Organizations (or staff) to be notified

- Applicable documents

- Preliminary schedule for the audit

The audit team leader shall sign and date each audit plan. Additionally, the lead auditor shall draft a notification memo from the *MANAGER, AUDITS,* to the affected project/program manager(s). The notification memo should summarize the information contained in the audit plan and include the plan as an attachment. Every effort should be made to notify affected parties, in writing, at least 30 days in advance of an impending audit. Affected parties include:

- Audit team members

- Program/project manager(s)

- Program/project immediate line manager(s)

- Program/project quality engineer

Checklists

Written checklist questions shall be developed for each audit prior to the beginning of the audit (opening meeting). These checklist questions shall act as a guide to the audit team in performing their investigation in order to assure that all important elements of the control system are examined. As such, they may be written in any format found to be useful to the individual auditor(s). They shall, however, include examination questions covering each control element specified in the audit base (requirements documents). Checklists shall be developed individually for each audit, but may include questions from previous audits and standard lists. To provide for added assurance that checklist questions are adequate for the audited area, each checklist shall be reviewed by a qualified lead auditor other than the preparer. This review shall be documented by the word *reviewed* and a signature and date somewhere on the front page of each checklist.

Performance

Each audit shall begin with a brief opening meeting between the audit team, management of the area to be audited, and affected quality engineer. Blank copies of the checklists to be used for the audit shall be distributed at the opening meeting. The audit shall be performed such that elements selected for examination are evaluated for conformance and effectiveness against specified requirements. Objective evidence shall be examined to the degree necessary to determine if the control elements are being implemented effectively. The results of this examination should be recorded on the checklist pages or on supplemental notes. Every effort should be made to keep the auditee apprised of the progress of the audit and concerns of the audit team.

Audit Report

Each audit shall conclude with a brief closing (exit) meeting between the audit team, management of the area audited, and affected quality engineer. Copies of the *DRAFT* audit conclusions (or summary), along with any *DRAFT findings* or *observations* should be provided to those in attendance.

Within one week of the audit closing meeting, the audit report shall be prepared in the form of a memo from the *AUDIT TEAM LEADER* to the *MANAGER, AUDITS*. The audit report shall contain the following information:

1. Audit title, number, and other identifying information.

2. Background information, such as audit purpose, scope, dates, audit team members, and procedures used. Also include a brief description of the activities audited and affected customers.

3. Summary and overall conclusions of the effectiveness of the quality program as implemented by the audited organization(s). Also include an executive summary of any *findings* or *observations* and how they affect the products or deliverables.

4. Listing of those who participated in the audit. This is normally presented as an attachment.

5. Specific *findings* or *observations* as attachments.

Audit *findings* shall be presented as a generic statement of the nonconforming condition followed by discussion (or explanation) points, the first of which should be a description of the specific requirement(s) for the control item under question. This should then be followed by three or more examples of specific objective evidence, found during the course of the audit, and supporting the conclusion that a nonconforming condition exists. To assist management in tracking and developing corrective action, each *finding* of an audit shall include audit identifying information (audit title and number), be sequentially numbered, and presented on a separate sheet of paper attached to the report.

Audit *observations* shall be presented in a fashion similar to audit *findings,* except that no requirement(s) information is necessary. Audit *observations* shall also be sequentially numbered and presented on a separate sheet of paper attached to the report.

The audit report shall be provided to the affected project/program manager(s) by a cover memo from the *MANAGER, AUDITS*. This cover memo shall forward the audit report and request corrective action as applicable. If the report includes any audit *findings,* a blank audit finding response form shall be included for use by the addressee. Generally, a response to an audit report should be requested such that a reply is received within 30 days of the audit exit meeting. Additional copies of the cover memo and report should be provided to other interested parties, the audit team members, and the audit files. If contract requirements dictate, a copy of the cover memo and report shall be provided to the affected customer.

Follow-Up

Responses shall be evaluated by the *AUDIT TEAM LEADER* for effective corrective action which addresses the concerns expressed by the audit report. Specifically, replies to audit *findings* shall be evaluated to verify that:

1. The cause of the problem has been identified.

2. Actions have been taken to correct the specific problem areas.

3. Actions to prevent recurrence have been identified.

4. Specific responsibilities and dates have been identified.

5. These actions have been or will be taken in a timely manner.

Once these have been obtained and any followup verification has been completed, the *AUDIT TEAM LEADER* shall complete the bottom of the audit finding response form to indicate that the audit *finding* has been closed.

Responses to audit *observations* shall be examined to see if the issues were evaluated for validity/applicability and potential improvement. If any corrective action response was indicated, it is advisable to verify that promised actions have been taken. The *AUDIT TEAM LEADER* shall document the acceptance of an audit *observation* response by the word *accepted* and signature/date in the margin of the response memo.

The *MANAGER, AUDITS,* shall be periodically apprised of the status of outstanding audit *findings* and *observations*. Appropriate steps, including involvement of the director of quality assurance, shall be taken to resolve outstanding audit issues.

Records

The following items are considered to be official audit records and shall be maintained by the *MANAGER, AUDITS* for five years:

1. Audit notification memo and audit plan

2. Blank audit checklists used

3. Audit report and forwarding memo

4. Audit response, including completed audit finding response forms

The following items are considered to be working audit records and shall be maintained by the *MANAGER, AUDITS,* for a period of one year, after which time they may be discarded:

1. Auditor/lead auditor qualification records

2. Completed audit checklists and auditor's working papers

3. Related miscellaneous correspondence

4. Annual audit schedules and any revisions

5. Quarterly audit schedules

6. Auditing procedures used

Forms

Examples of forms used in the administration of the audit program appear on pages 82–85. These may be modified at the discretion of the *MANAGER, AUDITS.*

- EXAMPLE -
AUDIT FINDING

Audit Title: _____ Audit No.: _____ Finding No.: ____

Finding: **Critical reviews of project deliverables are not being performed.**

Discussion

1. The QA Plan (QAP 19–23, rev. 3 of 2/10/88) requires that deliverable reports be subjected to internal peer review in accordance with Research Directive 601. RD 601 further requires that a listing of reviewed reports be maintained for the life of the research project.

2. The report *Effects of Snow on Road Surfaces* was not subjected to an internal peer review prior to its release.

3. Three reports (890–01, 07, 13) contained a listing of reviewers, but no records of comments and resolutions.

4. For the one report formally processed under the peer review system (Report #10), several reviewer's comments were significant. There was no record to show that these comments were resolved.

5. Customer letter 22–75 of 5/12/88 indicated serious shortcomings and reservations with the research results contained in Report #10.

AUDIT FINDING
RESPONSE FORM

Audit Title: _____ Audit No.: _____ Finding No.: ____

Finding:

Cause of the Problem:

Actions taken or planned to correct the individual items:

Actions taken or planned to correct the cause:

Responsibilities and timetable for the above actions:

Prepared by: _____ Date: _____

Reviewed by: _____ Date: _____
Remarks:

Is this Audit Finding closed? _____ When? _____
File with official audit records
Send copy to auditee

RECORD OF LEAD AUDITOR QUALIFICATIONS		
NAME: EMPLOYER:		DATE
QUALIFICATION REQUIREMENTS		CREDITS
EDUCATION - University/Degree/Date 　　　　4 credits max 　1. Undergraduate Level 　2. Graduate Level		
EXPERIENCE - Company/Dates 　　　　　　9 credits max 　Technical (0-5) and 　Specific Industry (0-1) 　Quality Assurance (0-2) 　Auditing (0-4)		
PROFESSIONAL ACCOMPLISHMENT - Date 　　2 credits max 　1. P.E. 　2. Society		
OTHER FACTORS 　　　　　　　　　　　2 credits max 　Explanation: 　Evaluated by: (Name & Title)　　　　Date		
Total Credits		
AUDIT COMMUNICATION SKILLS 　Evaluated by (Name & Title)　　　　　　　　Date		
AUDITOR TRAINING COURSES 　Course Title or Topic　　　　　　　　　　Date 　1. 　2.		
AUDIT PARTICIPATION 　Location　　　　　　　　Subject　　　　Date 　1. 　2. 　3. 　4. 　5.		
EXAMINATION　　　　　　　　Score　　　　Date		
AUDITOR QUALIFICATION CERTIFIED BY: 　(Signature and Title)　　　　　　Date Certified		
ANNUAL EVALUATION		

Signature				
Date				

LEAD AUDITOR QUALIFICATION FORM

AUDITOR TRAINING AND INDOCTRINATION

ITEMS REVIEWED:

1. The purpose of Quality Assurance and an audit.

2. The audit process, including preparation, performance, reporting, and closure.

3. Definitions of Audit Finding and Audit Observation.

4. Brief review of ANSI/ASQC Q1–1986.

5. Audit checklists and their use.

6. Orientation on the organization to be audited and affected projects.

7. Any special areas of concern.

ATTENDANCE:

Name	Organization

TRAINING CONDUCTED BY: _____ DATE: _____
Lead Auditor

APPENDIX 2

GLOSSARY OF TERMS

Appraisal
A form of the quality system audit, normally conducted to examine the total quality program effectiveness and implementation. An appraisal is usually conducted by a third party and reported to the highest levels of management.

Assessment
Another term for the quality audit, sometimes used to indicate a less formal means of measuring and reporting than the normal audit. An assessment is usually limited in scope.

Audit
An independent, structured, and documented evaluation of the adequacy and implementation of an activity to specified requirements. An audit may examine any portion of the management control spectrum, including financial, environmental, and quality aspects of business and government.

Audit Program
The documented methods used to plan and perform audits.

Audit Standard
A description of essential audit characteristics, reflecting current thought and practice.

Audit Team
A group of individuals conducting an audit under the direction of a team leader.

Auditee
The organization to be audited. The auditee may be another group within the firm/agency or it may be an entirely separate organization.

Auditor
A person who is qualified and authorized to perform all or part of an audit.

Certification (of auditors and lead auditors)
The act of determining, verifying, and attesting to the qualifications of a person to perform effective audits in accordance with applicable requirements. Certification may be internal (by the person's employer) or external (by a professional society such as the American Society for Quality Control or the Institute of Internal Auditors).

Characteristic
Any distinct property of an item or activity that can be described and measured.

Client
The person or organization requesting or sponsoring an audit. Typically, the client is the person within the quality group who is in charge of the audit program.

Confirmation
The agreement of data obtained from two or more different sources.

Corrective Action
Action taken to eliminate the causes of an existing undesirable condition, in order to minimize or prevent its recurrence.

Evaluation
The act of examining a process or group to some standard and forming certain conclusions as a result.

Examination
A measurement of goods or services to determine conformance to some specified requirement.

Finding
An audit conclusion which identifies a condition having a significant adverse effect on the quality of the goods or services produced. An audit *finding* is normally accompanied by several specific examples of the observed condition.

Follow-Up Audit
Verifies that some corrective action has been accomplished as scheduled, and determines that the action was effective in preventing or minimizing recurrence.

Guidelines
Methods which are considered good practice but which are not mandatory. Generally, the term *should* denotes a guideline and the term *shall* denotes a mandatory requirement.

Independent
Not directly responsible for the quality, cost, and/or production of goods and services being examined.

Inspection
Activities (such as measuring, examining, or testing) performed to determine conformance of one or more characteristics of a product or service to specified requirements.

Lead Auditor
A person who is qualified and authorized to manage and direct an audit.

Objective Evidence
Qualitative or quantitative information, records, or statements of fact which are based on observation, measurement, or test and which can be verified.

Observation
An audit conclusion which identifies a quality system weakness, either in definition or implementation. An audit *observation* identifies a condition which is not yet causing a serious degradation of quality.

Process Audit
The evaluation of a process operation against established instructions and standards. The process audit measures conformance of the processed item or activity to established standards. It also measures the effectiveness of process instructions. The audit is a check for adequacy and effectiveness of the process controls over the equipment and operators as established by procedures, work instructions, and process specifications.[1]

Product Audit
The examination, inspection, or test of a product which has been accepted previously for the characteristics being audited. Such an audit is a reinspection and retesting of the product which has already been accepted or a review of documented evidence of acceptance. It is an indicator of quality going to the customer.[2]

Quality Assurance
All those planned and systematic actions necessary to provide adequate confidence that a product or service will satisfy given requirements for quality.[3]

Quality Audit
A structured evaluation of controls affecting quality for effectiveness, adequacy, and implementation to predetermined standards.

Surveillance (see **Process Audit**)

Quality System Audit
A structured activity performed to verify that one or more portions of a quality program are appropriate and being implemented effectively in accordance with agreed-to standards of performance.

Quality (System) Survey
An activity conducted prior to a contract award and used to evaluate the overall quality capability of a prospective supplier or contractor.

Specification
A set of requirements to be satisfied by a product or service.

Standard
A government- or industry-endorsed description of essential characteristics of an item or activity. Standards may be product-specific (like ASCII for computer data exchange), user-specific (like MIL-Q-9858A for U.S. Defense Department Contracts), or generic (like ANSI/ASQC Q90 for Quality Management in general).

Verification
The act of reviewing, inspecting, testing, checking, auditing, or otherwise establishing and documenting whether items, processes, services, or documents conform to specified requirements.[4]

Footnotes

[1]Taken from information contained in *Quality Systems Auditor Training Handbook,* Programs Committee of the Energy Division, American Society for Quality Control, January 1986.

[2]Taken from information contained in *Quality Systems Auditor Training Handbook,* Programs Committee of the Energy Division, American Society for Quality Control, January 1986.

[3]Taken from *Quality Management and Quality Assurance Standards-Guidelines for Selection and Use* (ANSI/ASQC Q90–1987), American Society for Quality Control, June 1987.

[4]Taken from *Quality Systems Terminology* (ANSI/ASQC A3–1987), American Society for Quality Control, November 1987.

INDEX